BRIEF DISCOURSES ON THE GOSPEL

FOR

All Sundays and Festivals of the Year

TRANSLATED FROM THE GERMAN

OF

Rev. PHILIBERT SEEBÖCK, O.F.M.

BY

E. LEAHY

Frederick Pustet & Co.

Printers to the Holy Apostolic See and the
Sacred Congregation of Rites

NEW YORK   CINCINNATI

1916

Nihil Obstat.

REMIGIUS LAFORT, S.T.L.
Censor.

Imprimatur.

✢ JOHN CARDINAL FARLEY,
Archbishop of New York

New York, September 8, 1916.

Printed in U. S. A.

Copyright, 1916
in the U. S. and Great Britain
By FR. PUSTET AND CO.
New York and Cincinnati

FOREWORD TO TRANSLATION

It may be said with confidence that one of the most urgent needs of the Church in our day is the multiplication of short sermons. Hence it is a great pleasure to come upon such a treasury of excellent models and sources for brief talks from the altar as is given us in the volume of Father Philibert Seeböck, O.F.M., now translated into excellent English by E. Leahy. So much solid and useful matter is here set forth that it might serve as a basis, if need were, for much longer discourses than are named in the title. The tone and spirit of the little sermons are admirable: they are clear, practical and devout. It is to be hoped they will prove immensely useful to priests in charge of souls.

GEORGE O'NEILL, S.J., M.A.

MARCH 13, 1916.

TABLE OF CONTENTS

	PAGE
FOREWORD TO TRANSLATION	3

PART I

SERMONS FOR ALL SUNDAYS OF THE YEAR

INTRODUCTION

I. The Gospel of Our Lord Jesus Christ	9
II. The Ecclesiastical Year	16

ADVENT

I. Sunday of Advent:—Terrifying Signs which Shall Precede the End of the World	19
II. Sunday of Advent:—Herod—John in Prison	22
III. Sunday of Advent:—The Question for Advent	25
IV. Sunday of Advent:—John the Baptist Preaches Penance	27

CHRISTMAS

I. Sunday after Christmas:—The Prophecy of Simeon	32
I. Sunday after the Circumcision:—The Home at Nazareth	35
I. Sunday after the Epiphany:—Finding of the Child Jesus in the Temple	40
II. Sunday after the Epiphany:—The Marriage in Cana	44

III. Sunday after the Epiphany:—Prayer and Confidence..	49
IV. Sunday after the Epiphany:—The Storm on the Lake ..	52
V. Sunday after the Epiphany:—Wheat or Cockle	55
VI. The Church as the Grain of Mustard Seed and the Leaven....................................	59

LENT

Septuagesima Sunday:—Labor and its Reward...........	65
Sexagesima Sunday:—Fruit a Hundred Fold.............	66
Quinquagesima Sunday:—Healing of the Blind Man......	72
1st Sunday of Lent:—Temptations......................	76
2d Sunday of Lent:—The Transfiguration................	79
3d Sunday of Lent:—The Casting Out of a Dumb Devil...	83
4th Sunday of Lent:—Without God We Can do Nothing..	87
5th Sunday of Lent:—The Sin of Impenitence............	91
Palm Sunday:—Hosanna to the Son of David............	94

EASTER

Easter Sunday:—Easter Joy, Alleluia!...................	98
1st Sunday after Easter:—Our Lord's Easter Gift.........	102
2d Sunday after Easter:—The Good Shepherd............	105
3d Sunday after Easter:—Jesus at His Last Supper Consoles His Disciples....................................	110
4th Sunday after Easter:—Patronage of St. Joseph........	113
5th Sunday after Easter:—" Full " Joy in Prayer.........	116
6th Sunday after Easter:—Come, Holy Ghost!...........	120

PENTECOST

Whit Sunday:—The Gifts of the Holy Ghost.............	124
1st Sunday after Pentecost:—The Blessed Trinity, the Baptismal Vows.................................	127
2d Sunday after Pentecost:—The Great Supper...........	131
3d Sunday after Pentecost:—Feast of the Sacred Heart....	135

TABLE OF CONTENTS

	PAGE
4th Sunday after Pentecost:—All for Jesus	138
5th Sunday after Pentecost:—Wo to Him that Curses	141
6th Sunday after Pentecost:—Multiplication of the Loaves and Fishes	145
7th Sunday after Pentecost:—False Prophets	149
8th Sunday after Pentecost:—The Great Account	151
9th Sunday after Pentecost:—Jesus Wept	155
10th Sunday after Pentecost:—The Prayer of the Publican	158
11th Sunday after Pentecost:—Cure of the Man who was Deaf and Dumb	162
12th Sunday after Pentecost:—The Most Important Question of Life	165
13th Sunday after Pentecost:—Before and After Confession	169
14th Sunday after Pentecost:—Worldliness—Worldly Cares	173
15th Sunday after Pentecost:—The Angel of Death nd the Lord of Life	177
16th Sunday after Pentecost:—Sanctification of the Sunday	182
17th Sunday after Pentecost:—The Two Great Questions	186
18th Sunday after Pentecost:—Healing of the Man Sick with Palsy	190
19th Sunday after Pentecost:—The Happiness of Catholics	193
20th Sunday after Pentecost:—" Himself Believed and His Whole House "	197
21st Sunday after Pentecost:—How Ready God is to Forgive	201
22d Sunday after Pentecost:—" Render therefore to Cæsar the Things that are Cæsar's; and God the Things that are God's "	205
23d Sunday after Pentecost:—Remembrance of Death	209
24th Sunday after Pentecost:—Eternal Torments or Eternal Life	213

TABLE OF CONTENTS

PART II

FEASTS OF THE ECCLESIASTICAL YEAR

FEASTS OF OUR LORD JESUS CHRIST

	PAGE
Christmas Day:—The Crib at Bethlehem	218
The Circumcision (New Year's Day):—The Value of Time.	223
The Epiphany:—Gold, Frankincense and Myrrh	227
The Most Holy Name:—A Name above all Names	230
Easter Monday:—Jesus, our Companion through Life	234
The Ascension:—Until We Meet in Heaven	239
Whit-Monday:—The Excess of Divine Love	242
The Feast of the Dedication of Churches:—All Salvation is in Jesus	246

FEASTS OF THE BLESSED VIRGIN

The Immaculate Conception:—Mary, Our New Paradise	250
The Purification (Candlemas Day):—Mary Offers Her divine Son in the Temple	254
The Annunciation:—The Angelical Salutation	258
The Assumption:—The Best Part	262
Nativity of the Blessed Virgin:—Let us Rejoice at Mary's Happy Birth	266

FEASTS OF THE SAINTS AND MARTYRS

St. Stephen, First Martyr:—Witness for Christ	270
Saint Joseph:—Our Protector	274
Saints Peter and Paul:—The Princes of the Church	278
The Guardian Angels:—Devotion to Our Guardian Angels	281
All Saints:—Praise God in His Saints	284

PART I

SERMONS FOR ALL SUNDAYS OF THE YEAR

INTRODUCTION

The Gospel of Our Lord Jesus Christ

THE Greek word, Gospel, signifies a joyful message. By it we Christians understand the account, which indeed contains such glad tidings for us, of the Life and teachings of Our Lord Jesus Christ, of His glorious Resurrection and Ascension, and of His sending of the Holy Ghost upon the Apostles. Thus, the Gospel is the account of the sinful world's Redemption by the Eternal Son of God.

The Gospel contains all the truths and teachings of the Christian Faith and was written by the Evangelists, inspired by the Holy Ghost.

As the Catholic Church teaches, the Evangelists who preached the life and doctrines of Jesus Christ and who have left us the written account are: Matthew, Mark, Luke and John.

The four different Gospels, in reality, form but one which teaches us what we should do, and what we should not do, in order that we may attain salvation, and as heirs and co-heirs of Jesus Christ share with Him in His everlasting Kingdom.

Matthew, called Levi, one of the twelve Apostles, was the son of Alpheus; before his call to the Apostolate, he was a collector of taxes in the Roman custom-house on Lake Tiberias, and was very wealthy.

As he sat at the customs, our divine Lord saw him and said to him: "Follow me." And Matthew arose and followed Him.[1]

Obedient to the divine Master's call, he followed Him during the remainder of His public life, was a witness to His miracles and His Resurrection from the dead, and after the Ascension for fifteen years preached the doctrine of salvation in Judea.

Saint Matthew wrote his Gospel in Hebrew for the Jewish Christians as manifest proof that Jesus Christ was the promised Messiah. When

---

[1] Matt. ix, 9; Mark ii, 14; Luke v, 27. The last named adds: "And leaving all things, he rose up and followed him," Luke v, 28. By these words, we are to understand that he renounced all his wealth and became poor for Christ's sake.

INTRODUCTION 11

Christianity spread amongst the heathens, it was translated into Greek. He preached the Gospel in the countries south of the Caspian Sea, and suffering martyrdom, bore testimony with his blood to the divine truth of Christ's teachings.

John Mark was born in Jerusalem where his mother owned a house in which the first Christians used to assemble, and to which St. Peter repaired after his escape from prison. Probably it was he who converted Mark to Christianity, and it was for this reason that he called him his "son."[1]

Mark accompanied Saint Paul and Barnabas to whom he was related on their first missionary journey, but during the course of it, he separated from them. Saint Peter took him with him to Rome where he heard Peter preach; afterwards, as a lasting memorial, he wrote down these sermons for the Roman Christians, in Greek, it is true, for the learned, as St. Jerome and St. Augustine inform us. He was sent by Saint Peter as bishop to Alexandria where he labored with great fruit until the year 62 A.D. He consecrated Anianus as his successor, after which he returned to Rome where he shared St. Paul's first imprisonment. When the great persecution

---
[1] I. Peter v, 13.

of the Christians under Nero broke out, St. Mark returned to Alexandria, and there suffered martyrdom, being seized by the populace whilst celebrating the Divine Mysteries in a catacomb, and put to death by hanging. His holy body rests in the Church of St. Mark in Venice.[1]

Saint Luke was born in Antioch of heathen parents; he was a physician,[2] and after becoming a Christian, was a fellow-worker with Saint Paul whom he accompanied on his second missionary journey, and was the "only"[3] one who remained to assist him in his second imprisonment. Luke died in the 74th year of his age, a martyr for the teaching of Jesus Christ.

Saint Luke wrote the Gospel preached by Saint Paul proving in the clearest manner that Christ's doctrine of salvation was intended alike for Jews and pagans, and for the renewal of the whole human race which it should lead to salvation. His Gospel was written before the destruction of Jerusalem.

As a continuation of his Gospel, we also owe to Saint Luke the Acts of the Apostles in which is

---

[1] Rom. Martyrol., 31 Jan.
[2] Coloss. iv, 14, "Luke the most dear physician."
[3] "Only Luke is with me," II Tim. iv, 11.

INTRODUCTION

described the spread of the Church amongst Jews and heathens.

John, son of Zebedee, a Galilean fisherman, and of Salome, was a brother of James, surnamed "the Greater," who also followed the fisherman's calling. Salome was one of the women who contributed to the support of our Lord and His Apostles.

John was of a gentle, loving nature, yet at the same time, ardent and resolute. He was, at first, a disciple of the austere Baptist through whom he came to know our Lord. His first conversation with Jesus made such a deep impression on Saint John that he could not leave the new Teacher, and after the miraculous draught of fishes he became one of our Lord's disciples; later, our Lord chose him as an Apostle, and he was an eye and ear witness of all his divine Master's acts, works, miracles and teaching during the three years of His public life. As His beloved disciple, John was specially favored by our Lord in being present with Peter and James at the Transfiguration on Mount Thabor, and in being permitted to sit next his divine Master at the last Supper and to lean his head upon His breast. He was also privileged to stand at the foot of the Cross on Calvary, and to receive as His dying gift his Master's most Blessed Mother. After the death of our Lord, St. John was our Lady's faithful protector until she passed to Heaven.

After the Descent of the Holy Ghost, John remained for fifteen years in Jerusalem, at the end of which time he went to Asia Minor, taking up his abode in Ephesus from which city he exercised supervision over the Churches.

In the persecution of the Christians which broke out under Domitian, John was taken to Rome where, before the Latin Gate, he was plunged into a cauldron of boiling oil.[1] He was taken out uninjured, and was then banished to the island of Patmos.

Under the Emperor Nerva John was allowed to return to Ephesus where he died in the reign of the Emperor Trajan, being then nearly one hundred years of age. He was the only Apostle who did not die a violent death.

Saint Jerome tells us that "John, the Apostle, as the last of the Evangelists living, wrote his Gospel at the prayer of the Asiatic Bishops.

---

[1] On this spot now stands the Church of San Giovanni in Oleo.

INTRODUCTION 15

At that time, Cerinthus and other heretics, especially the Ebonites, were spreading the false doctrine that Christ had not been conceived of Mary. Thus it was necessary that the Apostle should testify to the divine origin of Christ.

Another reason was, that according to tradition, after reading the first three Gospels to the truth of which he testified, he had maintained that these should be limited to the last year of our Lord's life in which He suffered, the year after the imprisonment of John the Baptist.

But the Beloved Disciple himself tells us what was his chief aim in writing his Gospel.[1] "But there are also many other things which Jesus did: which if they were written every one, the world itself, I think, would not be able to contain the books that should be written."

The Gospel was written after Saint John's return from Patmos between the years 96-98 A.D.

It is a sublime testimony to the Divinity of Jesus Christ, as St. Augustine points out to us in the following striking passage:

"Of the four Gospels, or rather of the four books of one Gospel, that written by the Apostle,

---
[1] John xxi, 25.

St. John, who because of the keenness of his spiritual perception has been likened to an eagle, raises his proclamation to a far higher and more sublime elevation than that of the three others, an elevation to which he would raise our hearts also: For the three other Evangelists have each treated more of God made Man on earth than of His Divinity. But St. John, as if disdaining to stay on earth, has soared, not only above the earth, but above the choirs of angels, and above all the hierarchies of the invisible powers, and has attained to Him by Whom all things have been created, saying, "In the beginning was the Word—and the Word was God."

The Ecclesiastical Year

God who dwells in inaccessible light has created us that by knowing, honoring, and serving Him here on earth and by fulfilling His divine Will, we may share with Him in His Eternal Glory. To this end He has revealed Himself to us in His Works and in His Commandments, and in the Redemption purchased for us by His Only-Begotten Son Who is the Source of our sanctification.

Throughout the Ecclesiastical Year the Mysteries of our Religion are so apportioned that by means of the different circles of Feasts and Sundays, the Faithful may learn the whole doctrine of salvation, may rejoice in the divine Service of God, and may regulate their work and their lives according to the Christian Faith. Thus we learn during the Ecclesiastical Year what God has done to make us happy, and what we must do in order to merit that happiness.

In addition to the Sundays and the Festivals of our Lord are added the Feasts of our Lady and of the Saints who by following in the footsteps of Jesus Christ have left us an example of virtue, and thereby point out to us the road to Christian perfection.

The great divisions of the Ecclesiastical Year are: Christmas, Easter, and Pentecost.

Christmas

In this division are included the Sundays and Feast-days from the first Sunday of Advent to the Sixth Sunday after the Epiphany.

ADVENT

The word Advent signifies coming. The Church has appointed the four weeks of Advent as a time of preparation for the worthy celebration of the birth of our Lord Jesus Christ and of His Coming into our hearts. It is a time of penance, a time for contemplation, a time during which we should purify ourselves from those sins which most oppose the action of divine Grace within our souls. Of this the Church reminds us by the penitential violet of her vestments, by prohibiting participation in public amusements and gaieties, by the fasts which she prescribes, by the reading of the Gospel in which are foretold the signs which shall precede the Day of General Judgment and of that in which the Precursor of the Redeemer admonishes us to prepare the way of the Lord by worthily receiving the Sacraments of Penance and the Holy Eucharist.

First Sunday of Advent

Luke xxi, 25–33

Terrifying Signs which shall Precede the end of the World

> 25. "And there shall be signs in the sun, and in the moon, and in the stars: and upon the earth distress of nations, by reason of the confusion of the roaring of the sea and of the waves."
> Luke xxi, 25.

DEAR BRETHREN: What will be the amazement, the terror, of sinners when they behold the sun, as if to shut out the sight of men's crimes, go down veiled in darkness as in a mourning veil, in order to strike terror into them because during life they had abused the sunlight by walking in the paths of vice.

The moon shall no longer shine, but shall be the color of blood, "before the great and dreadful day of the Lord doth come" as the Prophet Joel [1] tells us. "Alas!" will the sinner cry out, filled with shame and terror, "I made use of the beautiful, beneficent moonlight, Heaven's gift, to defile my immortal soul with sin, and to commit loathsome deeds of darkness, instead of

---

[1] ii, 31.

bewailing my sins, like David, in the night-time, with floods of tears."

The stars which invite men to raise their eyes and hearts from earth to Heaven shall lose their brightness. "All creatures shall rise up and wreak vengeance on sinners because they have abused the works of God for the gratification of their passions."[1]

Wo! if the sun of divine mercy is also darkened for the sinner, if Mary, "fair as the moon,"[2] forsake him, and if in the heavens there no longer shine a friendly star, and if even his Guardian Angel, and all his holy advocates before God abandon his lost soul. " And he loved cursing, and it shall come unto him: and he would not have blessing, and it shall be far from him." [3]

But you say: "The Day of Judgment is still a long way off." Be it so. But the day of your death and particular judgment: is that still far off? May not death overtake you even this very day?

All the signs of the Day of Judgment shall be seen at the death of the sinner; never again shall his sad eyes behold sun, moon, or stars. As he

---

[1] St. Gregory the Great.
[2] Luke v, 6.
[3] Ps. cviii, 18.

lies on his bed of death, on his right hand the sinner shall behold all his past crimes which will drive him to despair; on his left, the Devil eagerly longing to seize his soul; beneath him yawns the abyss of Hell already open to swallow him into its depths for all eternity; above him, is the severe Judge Who is about to pronounce against him the irrevocable sentence of eternal damnation; behind his past life he sees the world which now rejects him; before his face is Death whose arrow transfixes his heart. Wherever he turns he finds nothing but terror and despair.

Dear Brethren, we shudder at the awful fate of a dying sinner. Let each one of us, therefore, avoid the least sin, for only then shall we guard ourselves from the same dreadful misery. O mortal man! each night, prepare thyself for death.

"Hear, O Lord, my prayer: give ear to my supplication in thy truth: hear me in thy justice. And enter not into judgment with thy servant: for in thy sight no man living shall be justified." [1]

"Sweet Jesus, be to me a Savior, and not a Judge." [2]—Amen.

---

[1] Ps. cxlii, i, 2.
[2] 50 days' indulgence each time, granted by Pius IX., 11 Aug., 1851.

Second Sunday of Advent

Matt. xiv, 2-10

Herod—John in Prison

1. Dear Brethren:

We read in to-day's Gospel that the greatest amongst the children of men, St. John the Baptist, so highly praised by our Lord Himself, lay bound in prison.

How did this happen? John had forbidden the licentious King Herod Antipas to marry his brother's widow, Herodias. "It is not lawful" he said fearlessly to the King "for thee to have her." These words caused him to be so hated that by the King's order he was thrown into prison and later was beheaded.

Even when languishing in prison John the Baptist did not retract what he had said, for to him the doing of the divine Will was more than kingly favor, than a place at the royal banquet, than splendid robes or a life steeped in luxury.

John spent his few remaining days on earth solely in promoting with all his power God's honor and the salvation of his fellow-men, more especially, of his disciples. Therefore, he sent

ADVENT

two of his followers to the divine Master to ask Him if He were the expected Messiah.

Now, dear Brethren, lift up your eyes to Heaven. Nineteen hundred years have passed since St. John the Baptist was released from the iron fetters which bound him as he lay in prison. And during all that long time, he has been immersed in an ocean of heavenly bliss whilst the proud, the cruel Herod during those nineteen hundred years has suffered the tortures of Hell. What vain remorse is his now, for not having heeded St. John's warning.

And, dear Brethren, if you are stiff-necked, if you grow angry when your pastors, your parents, or it may be true friends, tell you the truth and point out to you your faults, then you, too, will one day bitterly repent.

2. *Listen, my dear Brethren*, to the praise given by our divine Lord to His Precursor. Jesus said to the multitude, speaking of John "What went you out into the desert to see? a reed shaken with the wind?" "Did you think," says our Lord "when you went into the desert to see John that you would see a vacillating man, a man who like a weak reed would bend before men's threats and would let himself be moved by them, a man

who would waver in his belief that I am the Messiah?" Ah! no: John was not indeed such a man as this.

Dear Brethren, imitate St. John's example and be not like a reed shaken with the wind, do not, to-day, make good resolutions and to-morrow relapse into the old ways; do not, to-day, practise virtue and to-morrow countenance vice; do not in the morning with the Angels worship God in His Temple, and in the afternoon insult and blaspheme Him in the company of the wicked by every kind of sin. God will not be satisfied with such despicable vacillation. For He, your Creator requires your whole heart for Himself.

"Thou shalt love the Lord thy God with thy whole heart." He requires constant vigilance and the continual practice of virtue.

The foolish virgins were excluded from the Marriage Feast because they delayed until the last moment to provide themselves with oil. Ah! do not, like so many, put off practising virtue from one time to another, for then, as so often happens, it may be too late, and if you have not employed your talents, your time, your powers of soul and body for the honor and glory of your Creator and your God and for the salvation of your immortal soul you run the risk of being cast, like the bad servant, into outer darkness. Amen.

THIRD SUNDAY OF ADVENT
John i, 19–28

The Question for Advent
"*Who art thou?*" John i, 19.

1. "*Who art thou?*" As the Jews from Jerusalem questioned St. John by the river Jordan, asking him, " Who art thou?" so, on this, the third Sunday of Advent, to each and every one of us there comes the question: How have you prepared yourself, during this time, for the coming of Jesus into your souls? Have you by a contrite, candid confession purified your heart? Have you overcome some long and deeply-rooted sinful habit? Have you sanctified the Sunday both morning and evening and attentively listened to the Word of God? Have you said devoutly your morning and night prayers? Do you live in peace with your family and friends? Are you waiting to amend your life until you are on your death bed when Jesus Christ, the Judge of the living and the dead, is calling you before His Judgment Seat where He will no longer listen to

your prayers, if you are wanting in perfect contrition? Yes: who art thou, O man? If in your pride, you exalt yourself above others, remember, O mortal! that you are dust and into dust you shall return. How then can you, that are but dust and ashes, proudly exalt yourself? And with regard to your soul, how do you stand? Are you full of virtue and piety? Are you still, as you were after Baptism, a temple of the Holy Ghost or are you not rather groaning under the burthen of sin, a slave of the devil?

Are you a friend of God? Do you find your happiness in the frequent thought of Him and in doing all your actions with the intention of pleasing Him? Do you grieve, or are you indifferent when men boldly violate God's Commandments? Are you filled with charity towards your neighbor? Do you labor for his temporal and eternal welfare? Are you hard-hearted, unjust, passionate, unforgiving?

Question your conscience before Confession; question it every night before you retire to rest. How do you stand in the sight of God? How do you act towards your fellow-men? Are you a just man or a sinner? If to-day you were called to appear before the Judgment Seat of God, would you be worthy to be numbered amongst the elect, or would your place be amongst those who are condemned to eternal punishment? This is the question for Advent, the most important question of your life, upon the answer to which alone depends your eternal salvation. Let us now implore our divine Savior that when our last hour comes we may be able to give the right answer to this question. Amen.

Fourth Sunday of Advent

Luke iii, 1–6

John the Baptist Preaches Penance

> "preaching the baptism of penance . . ." Luke iii, 3.

1. *Do Penance.* Dear Brethren, if the Holy Precursor, John, were to come amongst us to-day, he would surely say to us, also: " Prepare ye the way of the Lord. . ." Hasten to purify your souls from sin by penance and a contrite heart, and by worthily approaching the Sacraments prepare for the spiritual birth of the divine Savior in your hearts that He may bless you with His divine grace and love. " Bring forth therefore fruits worthy of penance," he says to us, " for now the axe is laid to the root of the trees.

Every tree therefore that bringeth not forth good fruit, shall be cut down, and cast into the fire."

This is now the supreme moment, he tells you, for you to begin the amendment of your lives, and unless you do so, the most fearful punishments are reserved for you. From these words in the Gospel, dear Brethren, it is easy to conjecture what John the Baptist would preach to the hard-hearted rich, to the impure, to the drunkard, the passionate, the slothful in doing good, to the disobedient sons and daughters of these days.

The fruits of penance by no means consist merely of some devout practices. Sincere, earnest efforts to keep the Commandments of God and of the Church, to love God with our whole hearts, to imitate Jesus Christ, to love our neighbor as ourselves, and to fulfil faithfully the duties of our state in life: these are the real fruits of penance. The mere name of Christian will avail us just as little for salvation as their mere descent from Abraham will avail the Jews. As near as destruction is to the tree at whose roots the axe has already struck, so near are God's punishments to the man who is an unprofitable servant, who does no good works, particularly

ADVENT

if he audaciously continues to commit sin. To such sinners, Jesus Christ says: "Unless you do penance, you shall all likewise perish."[1]

2. *"Prepare ye the way of the Lord."*

"Every valley shall be filled." This is a parabolic mode of speech, to be understood in a figurative sense. If a king were about to visit his subjects who dwelt in a distant valley a thousand willing hands would be busy in cleaning the roads and removing every obstacle which might impede his journey. Shall we, dear Brethren, not take far greater trouble when we know that God, the supreme Lord of Heaven and earth, is coming to us at Christmas to bring us salvation and to bless us with His divine Presence?

If the roaring torrents of evil passions have torn up our hearts, leaving deep hollows or valleys, as it were, therein, we must fill these up with good works. When despondency, despair, begins to shake our hope in God's help and in His Providence, when we no longer find joy in prayer, when we grow weary of hearing the word of God, when sensuality, envy, hatred, inordinate desires wholly fill our hearts, then are those hearts of ours like unto a dark valley. We must fill up these

---
[1] Luke xiii, 5.

valleys with firm faith in the Providence of God without Whose Will not even a sparrow falls to the ground; with steadfast hope in the infinite Goodness of God Who ever helps those who trust in Him; with ardent love of God Who disposes all things for the good of those that love Him.

"Every mountain and hill shall be brought low." If pride, self-love, sensuality or any other sinful habit has become a mountain in our hearts, we must, by practising the virtue of humility, lay it low; we must learn more and more to know our weakness, and thus placing but little reliance on our own strength we shall trust all the more to God's assistance.

"And the crooked shall be made straight." If your thoughts, words, and works are not directed to God by a good intention, but have as their motive earthly desires and passions, then all that you do goes by crooked ways to an evil end. All your actions, your proceedings must be in accordance with God's Will and His Commandments outside which there is no happiness, no salvation.

"And the rough ways plain," that is to say, restitution must be made for all injury done to one's neighbor in his character or his goods. Ill-gotten goods must be restored and all enmity

must cease. All that is crooked and rough in our dispositions, in our words, and actions, unmercifulness, desire of revenge, quarrelling, wrangling: all must be made smooth.

Oh! dear Brethren, if we purify our hearts and wash away all stains of sin with tears of true repentance; if we adorn them with virtue, then like those in the time of John the Baptist we shall see the salvation of the Lord; we shall experience the sweet peace which Jesus brings.

CHRISTMAS

SUNDAY AFTER CHRISTMAS DAY

Luke ii, 23–40

The Prophecy of Simeon

> "Behold this Child is set for the fall, and for the resurrection of many in Israel."
> Luke ii, 34.

DEAR BRETHREN: In to-day's Gospel, we see the new-born Savior surrounded by pious souls who rejoice with holy joy at the great happiness which is their portion as the reward of their piety, their prayer, their visits to the Temple—the happiness of beholding the Savior and Redeemer of the world, of recognizing Him, and of receiving His blessing for Time and for Eternity.

The holy old man, Simeon, receiving into his arms from Mary the divine Child, raised his eyes to Heaven and cried aloud: "Now thou dost dismiss thy servant, O Lord, according to thy word in peace. Because my eyes have seen thy salvation." And then he spoke a great prophecy:

CHRISTMAS 33

1. *Jesus a stumbling-block.* Turning to Mary he said, " Behold this child is set for the fall, and for the resurrection of many in Israel, and for a sign which shall be contradicted."

Hence, to those Jews who will not acknowledge Him as the Messiah, who will not follow His divine teachings, the Savior will prove their eternal ruin and destruction. But the devout Israelites who, believing, receive Jesus Christ and observe His Law, will have a happy resurrection and will attain to Eternal Life.

Dear Brethren, to-day, also, this prediction of Simeon finds fulfilment amongst ourselves. But our Lord is not the cause of any man's damnation because He has given us so many means of preserving ourselves from such a fate. If a staircase is in good repair, easy of ascent and descent, we cannot lay the blame on it if a drunken man falls down and breaks his neck.

Do we wish that the Savior of the world should prove our eternal salvation rather than our eternal ruin? Let us, then, never separate from Jesus. Let us have no intercourse with the enemies of Christ who always resist the Son of God and His Church, both by false teaching and sinful lives. Beware of such! Jesus is set for their fall.

When you have to suffer contradiction or persecution in the cause of truth and virtue, seek consolation from Jesus. Here on earth virtue and vice are in perpetual conflict. As gold is tried in the furnace, so is the devout man's virtue proved when he bears his trials patiently. Temptations, the strivings of our evil passions are the touch-stone of virtue. At the side of the greatest Saints there ever stood a tempter, an enemy who strove to oppose him in his most pious practices, his holiest undertakings.

2. *A sword through Mary's soul.* " And thy own soul a sword shall pierce."

This prophecy was fulfilled to the letter. Mary's loving maternal heart suffered much indeed when the Jews insulted her divine Son and blasphemed against Him? But this most tender Heart suffered most, was pierced as if by a sword when she stood beneath the Cross and saw her beloved Son die the most terrible of deaths. Then she was submerged in an ocean of sorrow.

Oh! dear Brethren! Have compassion with our dearest Mother in her sorrows; ask her to obtain for you the grace of perfect contrition for all your sins which were indeed the cause of the Passion and Death of Jesus. Pray to her—O Mary! let the wounds of thine Immaculate Heart be deeply impressed on our hearts.

Dear Brethren, this is the last Sunday of the old year. Countless are the favors which God has bestowed on us during its course. Let us thank Him; let us ask pardon for all our sins; let us make a firm resolution to sin no more. My God, grant me the grace never to commit sin again. If we do this, then indeed, God will grant us all a happy New Year. Amen.

Sunday after the Feast of the Circumcision

Matt. ii, 19, 23

The Home at Nazareth

> "And coming he dwelt in a city called Nazareth."
> Matt. ii, 23.

Dear Brethren: The cruel King Herod being dead, God sent an angel into Egypt to Joseph, the foster-father of Jesus, to tell him that he might now return to his own country. "Arise," said the angel, "and take the child and his mother, and go into the land of Israel."

Joseph obeyed the divine command. With Mary and Jesus he undertook the long journey to the little town of Nazareth where the Holy Family dwelt for many years.

That home at Nazareth is to all time the model for every Christian home.

1. *It was a house of prayer*

Never from any spot on the wide earth did there ascend to Heaven prayer so fervent, so pleasing to God, as rose from that home at Nazareth. For that prayer ascended from the holiest hearts. In ecstatic delight the angels from the highest heavens looked down upon those who prayed, who at the first dawn of day offered to the Eternal Father their praise and their profoundest adoration.

My Brethren, it is your bounden duty to see that the practice of prayer is faithfully observed in your homes. Prayer is, indeed, one of the first duties enjoined by our holy Faith and strictly imposed upon us by God Himself. " You must pray always. Watch ye, and pray that you enter not into temptation." And the Apostles exhorted the first Christians who were saints and martyrs, saying,

"Be nothing solicitous; but in everything by prayer and supplication . . . let your petitions be made known to God."[1]

Pray, therefore, in your homes. Pray in the morning, at noon-day, in the evening; in all your needs call upon God for help. Pray with confidence, with perseverance; assembling together, unite in prayer. Parents, pray with your children, teach them to pray, that will be the best and finest inheritance you can leave them.

2. *It was a God-fearing home*

In that home at Nazareth were three souls filled with such fear of God as the world had never known, nor never will know: Jesus Christ Who consecrated to His heavenly Father every sigh of His divine Heart, every word that fell from His sacred lips, the most Immaculate Virgin, St. Joseph, her Spouse, who night and day walked in the Presence of God.

So, too, should your Christian homes be distinguished by the fear of God prevailing therein. "Fear God, and keep His commandments; for this is all man."[2] Where reigns the fear

---
[1] Phil. iv, 5.
[2] Eccles. xii, 13.

of God, there will be no bad language; you will find no evil deeds. Many, indeed, have the Crucifix in their homes, but often, in these houses there is little fear of God, and our Crucified Lord may look down upon the greatest excesses. It was the fear of God which preserved the chaste Susannah in the hour of her sorest trial. "But it is better for me to fall into your hands without doing it, than to sin in the sight of the Lord." [1]

3. *It was a home of love*

Who can describe the love which reigned in the home at Nazareth? The tenderest, holiest love existed between Mary and Joseph, and with what bonds of burning love were they united to Jesus, and Jesus to them!

True love should make happy every Christian home. [2] "This is my commandment, that you love one another, as I have loved you." These words concern wives, husbands, brothers, sisters, every member of the Home. Happy the home where reigns this love, in it all crosses are lightened, all tears are dried. On such a home

---

[1] Daniel xiii, 23.
[2] John xv, 12.

God showers His blessings, and His holy angels, guarding it, spread their wings over it. But, on the other hand, how sad when holy love is wanting in a Christian home!

The Holy Family were filled with love for strangers also. Although poor themselves and living by the labor of their hands, yet never was their house closed to those in trouble, everyone in sorrow found consolation there, to everyone hungry was given bread.

Dear Brethren, if it should happen that you receive no thanks from those whom you have benefited, do not grow weary of doing good, but hope for two-fold reward from God.

Conclusion. Often contemplate the holy Home of Nazareth as your model of prayer, of the fear of God, of Christian Charity. And you will thereby merit to be received one day into the abode of eternal bliss, where you will share with the Holy Family, Jesus, Mary, and Joseph, in the Glory of Heaven for all eternity. Amen.

First Sunday after the Epiphany

Luke ii, 42-52

Finding of the Child Jesus in the Temple

"Did you not know that I must be about my father's business?" Luke ii, 49.

DEAR BRETHREN: How beautiful is to-day's Gospel in which our divine Lord in His ineffable goodness, whilst as yet only in the twelfth year of His sacred humanity, becomes our Teacher. Let us contemplate Him as He appears in two scenes in Jerusalem and in Nazareth, and we shall thereby learn and recognize:

I. The zeal of Jesus for the honor of His heavenly Father.

II. The obedience of Jesus to His earthly parents.

Let us go then to the school of the divine Master that we may learn from Him Who is the Son of God true wisdom and knowledge of our eternal salvation.

I. ZEAL

How beautiful the example given to us by the Holy Family. Mary did not claim that exemption from the Law to which, by right, she was entitled "And his parents went every year to

Jerusalem." And thus, once more, they journeyed there in faithful observance of God's Law, this time accompanied by the divine Child.

How edifying it is to see the father and the mother of a family united in their devotional exercises and assisting together at the Sunday Mass. How willingly the children join them in their devotions, and thus from early youth become habituated to the practices of religion.

But Jesus remained longer in the Temple. His love for His Heavenly Father urged Him yet more strongly than the ties which bound Him to Mary and Joseph! "They found Him in the Temple." Ah! how few young people there are who imitate this beautiful example of zeal for God's Honor. How many of them shun going to the Church; even on Sunday scarcely can they wait for Mass to be finished when they rush out; they never think of attending the afternoon or evening devotions; during the week, even if they have time, they never enter a church. And yet these young people have time to go to dances, to theaters, to picture-houses; they have time to play bridge, to keep dangerous company.

Alas! for such young people! What will become of them? Now, in their youth, they forget God, they despise His Commandments. In later years God will forget them, will despise them. He will withdraw the light of His grace from these unhappy souls. In the darkness of their evil passions they will fall deeper and deeper into sin until at last they die unrepentant. O divine Redeemer! O most loving Jesus, preserve the youth of the present day from such awful folly.

II. OBEDIENCE

Now let us journey with Jesus, Mary and Joseph back to Nazareth. What does the Gospel tell us concerning the life of the Son of God in Nazareth during the years which elapsed from the twelfth to the thirtieth year of His age? Perhaps, like earthly princes, those years were spent in the pursuit of sport and pleasure. Ah, no! the Son of the Eternal Father was obedient to two of His creatures. He "was subject to them." Those years of His life were spent in the lowliest toil, in a carpenter's workshop. You, sons and daughters of Christian parents, will you continue to grumble, to complain, to refuse obedience to your father and mother? Contemplate that life at Nazareth during all those long years, and then in the light of that divine example, reflect, dust and ashes, as you are, on your behavior in your home.

Jesus Christ, the second Adam, by His obedience at Nazareth and even unto death on the Cross atoned for the disobedience of Adam in the Garden of Eden, and for the disobedience of all his descendants who transgress the commandments of God. And thus the divine Master teaches rebellious man that only by obedience to God and His representatives on earth can he regain the way which leads to Paradise.

Jesus Christ became obedient, He to Whom the whole universe belongs, and before Whom the angels, veiling their faces in awe, fall prostrate and adore.

Christian sons and daughters, if you would have a long and happy life, if you wish God's blessing on your earthly pilgrimage, obey your parents and superiors. For the fourth Commandment requires you to yield this obedience. Be obedient, then, to your earthly parents; be zealous for the honor of your heavenly Father. And implore of Jesus that like Him, you, also, as you grow in years, may grow in grace and wisdom before God and man. Amen.

Second Sunday after the Epiphany

John ii, 1–12

The Marriage in Cana

> "This beginning of miracles did JESUS in Cana of Galilee: and manifested his glory, and his disciples believed in him."
> John ii, 11.

DEAR BRETHREN: The Son of God would not have honored the marriage feast at Cana with His divine presence if the bridal pair had not been good, virtuous people. They must have had a great personal love for our Lord, since they valued so highly His presence and that of His blessed Mother and His disciples and made them so welcome. And how richly did Jesus reward them for their invitation! For their supply of wine running short, He worked a miracle to remedy the deficiency.

Let us, also, in all our undertakings, our business, our joys, our sorrows, take care that Jesus shall be with us. Let us do nothing without Him; let everything be done with Him and for Him. Thus shall we always experience His all-powerful assistance.

That we may thoroughly recognize this most consoling truth, let us take from to-day's Gospel for consideration two points only.

I. The omnipotence of the divine name of Jesus.

II. The Blessed Virgin's intercession.

I. JESUS

St. John tells us that at this marriage feast our Lord said to the servants, "Fill up the waterpots with water. And they filled them up to the brim." Therefore it was not to His disciples that our Lord intrusted the carrying out of His orders, but to the servants of the house that so there might be no room for suspicion. Thus does God ever come to the assistance of our weak faith so that we must say with the psalmist "Thy testimonies are become exceedingly credible."[1] "Draw out now," said the divine Master, "and carry to the chief steward of the feast." The latter who was an expert, a connoisseur in wines, when he tasted this water turned into wine found that it was the best yet produced at the feast.

Dear Brethren, above all things this touching

---
[1] Ps. xcii. 5.

miracle should confirm and strengthen in our souls as it did in the hearts of the disciples our living faith in the divinity of Jesus Christ Who has by it so gloriously shown His Omnipotence. Yes: adhere steadfastly to your holy Faith and trust firmly to the Almighty power of your Christ. As good Christians do —not what the desires of the flesh, the lust of the eyes suggest to you,—but whatsoever things Jesus commands you to do, if you would find happiness even in this life, and would die a holy death.

Now, my Brethren, remember that amongst the early Christians, at all festive entertainments the utmost decorum and sobriety prevailed; the conversation was always edifying, and before and after the repasts prayers were said and hymns sung. At the present day, how different is the behavior at many entertainments. People sit down to table without asking God's blessing on themselves and the gifts which He has given them, and they go away without returning Him thanks for those good things which they have received from His bounty. How often is the conversation indulged in at these repasts of a scandalous nature. How many festive gatherings, how many weddings are disgraced, dishonored by sinful revelling, disorderly conduct, as if it were impossible to combine amusement with seemly behavior. Certainly at such assemblies as these where order and Christian decorum have no place we shall not find Jesus Christ.

II. MARY

In what a beautiful light does our dear Lady, the Mother of God, appear at this marriage feast of Cana. How sweet, how amiable her action. Perceiving that the wine ran short, the Mother of Jesus said to Him: "They have no wine."

O most Holy Mother, with good reason does the Church salute thee: "O clement, O loving, O sweet Virgin Mary!" No sooner didst thou perceive the want, the embarrassment of the host at this marriage feast than thou didst hasten by thy tender intercession with thy divine Son to obtain help and relief.

My dear Brethren: If in the midst of the many dangers to which you are daily exposed in soul and body you should feel afraid; if you feel yourselves powerless to resist your overpowering inclination to evil; if you have no love of God in your hearts; if you find no joy in prayer; then, after the example of so many Saints, turn to Mary, the all-powerful Advocate with Jesus Who will, certainly, never refuse her request.

But, in order that you may the more surely obtain the intercession of the Mother of Mercy with her divine Son, honor her by your pious practices: the devout repetition of the Angelus, three times a day, the daily recital of the Rosary, the reception of the Sacraments on her great Feasts. And as she said to the attendants at the marriage feast of Cana, "Do what he tells you," so, also, she says to us: "Keep my Son's Commandments; be not ashamed of His Name—then, shall I plead for you with Him, and obtain from Him all that you want."

Thus, dear Brethren, after our earthly pilgrimage is ended, may we through the intercession of Mary and the Almighty Power of Jesus Christ be admitted, rich in good works, to the Eternal Marriage Feast where we shall enter into the Glory of Jesus and Mary.

Third Sunday after the Epiphany

Matt. viii, 1–13

Prayer and Confidence

> "But let him ask in faith, nothing wavering..."
> James i, 6.

DEAR BRETHREN: How tender, how merciful, how compassionate is our divine Savior! In to-day's Gospel we see how He completely restored to health two persons who were afflicted with incurable disease, thus rewarding by a miracle their lively faith and confidence in prayer. Let us, therefore, learn to-day from these miracles in all our necessities to have recourse to God by prayer with confidence that He will assist us. This is the lesson taught us:

1. *By the Leper.* This poor sufferer's first act was to adore our Lord, thereby showing his faith in His Almighty Power, then he earnestly implored His help: "Lord, if thou wilt, thou canst make me clean." And then, our divine Lord, stretching forth His hand, touched him, saying: "I will, be thou made clean." And forthwith his leprosy was cleansed.

Dear Brethren: Leprosy is an image of mortal sin. You would take the greatest care to guard yourself from contact with a leper; you would scrupulously avoid all intercourse with him. But you have far greater reason to fly, to be filled with terror at the approach of a person who may lead you into sin, or at finding yourself in surroundings likely to prove the occasion of sin.

O my God, grant us the grace to recognize clearly that it would be better to die a thousand times than to commit one mortal sin.

Like this happy leper who was healed, ever take refuge with Jesus Who can and always will help us if we pray to Him with confidence and perseverance. To cleanse your soul from the leprosy of sin, go to Jesus in the tribunal of Penance; acknowledge your sins to the priest who is God's representative, and make a firm resolution to avoid those sins into which you habitually fall and to strive to correct your predominant passion, and then you will return to your home purified from all sin.

2. *By the Centurion.* Although by birth and education a heathen, the centurion was a very good worthy man and a model of true charity. He could not do more for his own son than he did for his poor servant whom sickness had rendered useless to him. Mark well, dear Brethren, that

those who show mercy to others will in their turn obtain mercy from God.

With what confidence this centurion went to our Lord and begged help for his servant who was stricken with palsy. And then with what humility he said: " Lord, I am not worthy that thou shouldst enter under my roof; but only say the word, and my servant shall be healed."

At once, our divine Savior rewarded his faith, and there and then healed the man who lay sick at a distance. Listen to our Lord's words:[1] " Have the faith of God. Therefore I say unto you, all things whatsoever you ask when ye pray, believe that you shall receive; and they shall come unto you." For this reason St. James the Apostle also exhorts us;[2] " But let him ask in faith, nothing wavering. For he that wavereth is like a wave of the sea, which is moved and carried about by the wind." According to the measure of our faith will be the measure of God's assistance, " believe that you shall receive; and they shall come unto you."

Dear Brethren: Jesus Christ is "yesterday, and to-day, and the same for ever."[3] Go then to Him in all your necessities of soul and body. The

---
[1] Mark xi, 22, 24.   [2] James i, 6.   [3] Heb. xiii, 8.

greater your faith and confidence, the more abundant will be the help you shall receive.

O most loving Jesus, increase our faith and confidence. Amen.

Fourth Sunday after the Epiphany

Matt. viii, 23, 27

The Storm on the Lake

> "Lord save us, we perish."
> Matth. 8, 25.

Dear Brethren: He who journeys with Jesus Christ will surely reach the right goal. We learn this most consoling truth in to-day's Gospel. On one occasion, after having preached to a multitude of people on the shore of the Sea of Galilee, our divine Savior commanded His disciples to cross to the country of the Gerasians on the opposite shore. In this voyage of our Lord and the storm which burst over the Lake together with the miraculous deliverance of the disciples at the word of their divine Master, we see:

I. An image of man's life.
II. A prototype of the Church.

I. THE BARK OF LIFE

We are all sailing on the sea of this world; we are voyaging in a frail vessel, exposed to the treacherous elements, to many dangers which threaten soul and body; we are steering from this earthly shore across to the one on the farther side. Well for us if we have Jesus with us in our vessel; if we carry Him in our hearts, He will be our Captain; His Providence will direct our helm; His word will be our compass and guide; Faith will be our sail, Hope our anchor, the Sacrament of Penance our flag; our mast the Cross; the Adorable Sacrament of the Altar will be our sustenance and Heaven the blessed goal, the haven of rest, which we must ever keep before our eyes.

Dear Brethren: On your voyage to the shores of eternal bliss you have to encounter so many storms, such raging billows, so many pirates, so many sunken rocks any of which may wreck your frail vessel. On the sea of this world you run greater danger of losing your soul than you do of losing your life. Call, therefore, day and night, on your divine Savior "Lord save us, we perish."

"Lord"!   We implore Thine Almighty Power; all Nature must obey Thee.

"Save." We trust in Thy Mercy, Thou wilt save us.
"Us." We pray for all, for ourselves, for one another.
"We perish." Without Thee, O Lord Jesus Christ, we can do nothing good.

God permits His own to be in need that they recognize in Him their one and only Helper.

II. THE BARK OF THE CHURCH

In the foundation and the preservation of His Church, Jesus Christ most especially manifested His Omnipotence and His miraculous assistance. He Himself, the Founder of this Church, died nailed to the Cross, and His frightened disciples were dispersed. Who, at that time, would have believed that a new Religion founded under such circumstances could flourish. And yet it was precisely through His death that Jesus Christ established and fortified His Church. "And I, if I be lifted up from the earth, will draw all things to myself." [1]

In all ages the Church of Jesus Christ has suffered persecution. The blood of Christians shed for the Faith has flowed in rivers. But, behold, the Almighty Power of Jesus Christ! "The blood of the Christians has become fresh seed for the propagation of the Faith. The more

---

[1] John xii, 32.

Christians you put to death, the more spring up again." [1]

2. Speaking of the Church, St. Bernard says beautifully: "In the beginning the Church wept over the death of the Martyrs, still more did She weep at the separation from her, through error, of so many of her numbers. She weeps, more than all, over the scandal caused by her bad children."

We, dear Brethren, desire to be good children of our holy Mother the Church, and by our lives and our obedience to her commandments to console her in her sorrow.

O loving and Omnipotent Jesus, guide us all in the bark of the Church Militant safely through all storms to the shore of eternal happiness, Amen.

Fifth Sunday after the Epiphany

Matt. xiii, 24–30

Wheat or Cockle

> "Gather up first the cockle, and bind it into bundles to burn, but the wheat gather ye into my barn."
>
> Matt. xiii, 30.

DEAR BRETHREN: Our Lord seated on board a little fishing vessel moored close to the

---

[1] Tertullian.

landing place on the sea of Galilee, proposed this beautiful parable to the multitude assembled on the shore. Let us consider what is the truth which we are to learn from this parable: whether we ourselves are to be accounted as good seed, as wheat, or as cockle. It is a question of whether we are to be garnered into the Heavenly barns or cast into Hell-fire.

I. WHEAT

According to His own explanation, the sower is Jesus Christ Himself Who gives to us the pure, fruitful, divine Truth which alone can save us, the good seed which through His Church He is ever scattering over the field of the world. The fruits of this seed, the harvest, the wheat, are those good Christians who, believing, accept the teachings of Jesus Christ, preserve them pure, and faithfully follow them. Thus, every pious, virtuous Christian is the fruit of the good seed sown by our divine Redeemer. Oh! how dear, how precious is this fruit to the Son of God. To Him the honest peasant, the upright mechanic, the God-fearing poor, are far dearer than the proud rich, than the prince on his splendid throne who does not fulfil his duties as a Christian.

We thank Thee a thousand times, O merciful Savior, for all Thy graces which as heavenly seed Thou dost scatter in the souls of men. As the sun shines upon the whole world giving heat and light to every creature, without one single exception, so with the fire of Thy divine grace Thou dost warm and enlighten every man who does not withdraw himself from Thy love.

Every holy thought, every good disposition, every victory over evil passions, every desire of amendment, every firm resolution to lead a pious life: these are Thy work, O Jesus, the effect of Thy grace, the precious fruit of Thy Passion and Death.

But alas! whilst men slept, the enemy came, sowed cockle among the wheat, and then went away.

II. THE COCKLE

1. Who are those whom our Lord designates as cockle? "The children of the wicked one," as He tells us Himself, who have caused scandals, and have worked iniquity in His kingdom.

The enemy who in the night-time sowed the cockle is the devil, God's Arch-enemy, who deceived our first mother Eve, and has never ceased striving to lead her children into sin. Satan still continues to work iniquity. He is ever going about like a hungry, roaring lion seeking whom he may devour. He cannot force you to commit sin, but he can try to tempt you into doing so.

Watch, therefore, dearly beloved Brethren, that you may not be seduced from your Faith, or enticed into committing mortal sin, which may easily happen if you are proud, if you think that you know better than the holiest, the most learned men; if you read bad books; if you keep company with those who scoff at Religion; above all, if you, yourself, lead a sensual, irreligious life. For pride and evil passions have ever been the cause of unbelief.

Pray, therefore, very fervently, because without God's assistance no one can obtain the victory over the enemies of his salvation.

Always remember your last end. God will command His Angels to gather the cockle and to cast it into the fire in which it shall burn during all eternity. But the wheat—the Just—shall shine like the sun for ever in the Kingdom of the Father, "He that has ears to hear, let him hear."

O Jesus, divine Sower! strengthen us against the countless temptations of the world that we may, one day, be gathered, as pure wheat into the granaries of Thy Kingdom of eternal bliss, Amen.

Sixth Sunday after the Epiphany

Matt. xiii, 31–35

The Church as the Grain of Mustard Seed and the Leaven

> "The Kingdom of Heaven is like to a grain of mustard seed."
> Matt. xiii, 31.

Dear Brethren:

Our divine Savior proposed the two beautiful parables of the Mustard seed and the Leaven to the people on the shore of the Sea of Galilee. He would by these parables show how His Church, which was to bring salvation to the world, by means of its inherent divine power would develop externally whilst at the same time operating and manifesting its activities within. And thus Our Lord willed by these parables more especially to prevent His disciples becoming discouraged when they saw how slowly the divine doctrine spread in the beginning.

I. THE GRAIN OF MUSTARD SEED

I. As the little grain of mustard seed of all garden-plants grows into the tallest shrub, so the

Church of Jesus Christ from the smallest beginnings has grown into the kingdom of God which has spread over the whole world.

How marvelous has been this growth. Twelve poor fishermen preaching a Man God Crucified change the whole earth, and establish a Religion which declares war against the ideas, the desires, the sensuality, and all the principles of the heathen world. By means of these twelve poor men without power, without money, without eloquence, Jesus Christ caused the seed of the Christian Religion to be sown.

And what a mighty tree has grown from this seed notwithstanding the persecutions by Jews and heathens which the Christians endured, offering no resistance save that of silence and patience even unto martyrdom.

Speaking of the first Christians Saint Augustine says thus beautifully: "They were bound in chains; they were tortured; they were scourged; they were put to death. And yet they ever increased in number."

Dear Brethren: Never cease to preserve within your hearts a strong and lively faith in the divine origin of the Catholic Church which was founded by Jesus Christ. And at the same time strive that you, yourselves, may spring up in this garden of God on earth like the grain of mustard seed into a great tree, in order that you may bring forth fruits of eternal life.

It is from small and insignificant beginnings that all good develops in the heart of man, and only by degrees do the germs of goodness grow into perfect virtue. And it is the same with evil. If you despise little things, if in small matters you are untruthful, dishonest, if you do not resist your inclination to speak ill of your neighbor, if you do not curb sensual desires and observe modesty in dress and in speech, then, surely will evil grow strong within you, and you will become evil men, and like unfruitful trees will be cut down and cast into the fire. Oh! strive to avoid everything which has the least appearance of evil.

II. THE LEAVEN

1. The parable of the Leaven indicates, in the first place, the great change wrought by the Christian Religion in man's life.

A little leaven mixed with a quantity of meal, by means of its acidity, gradually changes the color, taste, and smell of the meal, and renders it more nutritious. So with the Religion of

Jesus Christ. Wherever it spread it manifested clearly its divine power by transforming those who embraced it into splendid Christians, models of virtue and holiness.

The heathens, blind worshippers of false gods, filled with superstition, believers in absurd fables, were enlightened; they adored the true God, and overcoming the shameful vices in which so many of them were steeped, they led the holiest of lives. Even youths and tender maidens, mere children, in the fiercest persecutions remained true to their faith in Jesus Christ, the Son of God and the Savior of the world.

Dear Brethren, it is thus that the Religion of Jesus Christ must permeate our entire being that so we may turn away from everything sinful and lead holy lives. Yes: our every word, our every act must be directed to God, must be sanctified. Such is the example set before us in the lives of the Saints of God of every age and of every rank and condition.

St. Augustine, who before his conversion was wholly immersed in sensuality and worldly pleasures, happened to be present at a sermon preached in Milan by Saint Ambrose who read the following passage from St. Paul's Epistle to the Romans.[1] "Let us walk honestly as in the day: not in rioting and drunkenness, not in chambering and impurities, not in contention and envy: But put ye on the Lord Jesus Christ, and make not provision for the flesh in its concupiscences." These words effected a sudden change in Saint Augustine's dispositions; he begged for admittance into the Church and by his learning and sanctity afterwards became one of her most brilliant lights.

Thus, all the teachings of the Christian Religion have a divine force by which they can make us pleasing to God here on earth and eternally happy hereafter.

O most merciful Jesus, grant that Thy divine teachings may penetrate our whole being that thus we may grow in the knowledge of Thy holy Religion, and may one day enjoy for all eternity the fruits of our labors here on earth. Amen.

B. THE SEASON OF LENT

The great Festival of Easter is the culminating point of all the feasts of the Ecclesiastical year. For "if Christ be not risen again, then is our preaching vain, and your faith is also vain."[2]

---

[1] C. xiii, 13–14.   [2] Cor. xv, 14.

This Feast is also the pledge of our own eternal glorification. "For if the dead rise not again, neither is Christ risen again."[1]

But, in order that we may participate in the glorification of our divine Redeemer, it is absolutely essential that we should renounce all sensual pleasures and labor to effect a complete renewal of our lives. Therefore, as a preparation for the Festival of Easter, the Church has instituted the season of Lent which lasts from Septuagesima Sunday until Palm Sunday and includes Holy Week. During this time, the purple vestments, the omission of the Gloria in the Mass and the silence of the organ serve to remind us that if we would be purified from sin and celebrate with Christ a spiritual resurrection we must be sincere and earnest in doing penance.

---

[1] Ibidem 16.

LENT

Septuagesima Sunday

Matth. xx, 1-16

Labor and Its Reward

> "Go ye also into my vineyard . . ." Matt. xx, 7.

DEAR BRETHREN: On this Sunday the Holy Sacrifice of the Mass begins with the words of the Psalmist: " The sorrows of hell encompassed me: and the snares of death prevented me. In my affliction I called upon the Lord, and I cried to my God:" [1] Would that the Church's grief and lamentations might pierce the hard hearts of sinners, that thus during these days whilst it is yet time, before those tears shall be shed for them in vain, before it is too late, they might forsake their evil ways. Would that they might labor diligently at the all important work of repentance and amendment which to-day's Gospel most emphatically enjoins upon us.

---
[1] Ps. xvii, 6, 7.

I. LABOR

Our divine Savior likens Himself to a householder who goes forth in the early morning and at every subsequent hour of the day to hire laborers for his vineyard. Oh! give thanks to God that He has called you by Baptism in preference to so many millions to be a member of His Church. But, we must remember that it is not merely a question of membership with the Church. For, if we, as Catholics, do not follow the teachings of the Gospel, our having been called by God to be members of His Church will but serve to sink us deeper into hell.

The divine Householder does not grow weary of going forth at the various hours of the day to hire laborers—in their youth, their manhood, their old age—for His vineyard. But labor diligently at the work of your salvation. For you know not the day nor the hour when the Lord will come. How many are but idlers to whom all that concerns the service of God, prayer, hearing the Word of God, frequenting the Sacraments, is abhorrent. They are ungrateful to God Whose talents they bury; they are their own enemies, for they risk their eternal salvation. Dear Brethren: Listen to the words of warning

addressed to you by the Apostle St. Peter.[1]
"Wherefore, brethren, labor the more, that by good works you may make sure your calling and election. For doing these things, you shall not sin at any time."

II. REWARD

"And when evening was come, the lord of the vineyard saith to his steward: Call the laborers and pay them their hire, beginning from the last even to the first."

Dear Brethren: For us too the evening will come. After death every diligent laborer will receive from Jesus Christ that reward which he merits, will receive it in full measure pressed down and overflowing. "Rejoice and exult for great is your reward in the kingdom of heaven." Do not grow weary, therefore, in doing good. Sooner than you think for, you will strike the joyful hour when you shall receive eternal and richest recompense.

How the weary laborer who has borne the heat and burthen of the day rejoices when the star of evening shines in the heavens and he receives his reward, and can rest. So too the devout Christian

[1] II Peter, i, 10.

who has spent his life in constant toil, in pain, in suffering, accepting all these things as God's wise dispensations in his regard, is glad when comes the close of his life. May we thus spend all the days of our lives, then will the evening of those lives be for us fair and joyous. Dear Brethren: Our reward is not measured by the length of time, but by the diligence, the love, the loyalty, the humility with which through the grace of God we labor. The laborers who came last received as much reward as those who were hired first, because they were more diligent and thus made up for those hours during which they were idle. He who repents and is converted late in life, by the greatness of his love can merit the same reward as the servant of God who has labored from his youth.

Our divine Lord concludes to-day's Gospel with these solemn words: " Many are called, but few chosen." Therefore, Brethren, strive with all your strength to enter in at the narrow gate. For " many, I say unto you, shall seek to enter in, and shall not be able." [1] Amen.

---

[1] Luke xiii, 24, 25.

Sexagesima Sunday

Luke viii, 4–15

Fruit a Hundred Fold

> "And other some fell upon good ground; and being sprung up yielded fruit a hundred fold."
> Luke viii, 8.

DEAR BRETHREN: To you it is given to understand the secrets of the kingdom of God. Jesus Christ, the divine Sower, is ever going out to sow the seed of the Word of God in the Church, and to hear this Word of God and to receive it, is as necessary for our souls as food is for our bodies. But, as our Lord Himself tells us, for many the seed is sowed in vain, so that they do not believe, do not grow holy.

Now, to-day, let us briefly consider three questions, that we may from every sermon, that is to say, from the seed of the divine Word, bring forth fruit a hundred fold.

I. What does it mean to hear the Word of God with "a good and upright heart"? You hear the Word of God with "a good and upright heart" when you go to the Church with the pure intention of learning to know better the Will of God and His Commandments, in order that you may imitate more closely your divine Savior, and may render still more secure your eternal salvation. Therefore, leave all your worldly cares and pre-occupations outside the Church door; quietly, in the Presence of God, collect your thoughts; implore the Holy Ghost to enlighten you and make an act of contrition for all your sins. For the divine Spirit cannot enter into a sinful soul.

Before the sermon, it will be very salutary if in your heart you pray thus to God: My God, remove from me all worldly thoughts that thus Thy divine Word may not in my heart fall upon rocks or amongst thorns. Grant Thy blessing to this sermon that I may derive great profit from it.

II. What does it mean to keep the Word of God in your hearts?

Dear Brethren: The seed must not remain lying on the surface of the earth; if it is to bring forth fruit, it must sink deep into the ground and be covered. So with the Word of God. The mere listening to it will not suffice, nor will it do to apply what you hear to others. You must let the Word of God sink deeply into your heart, you must keep it hidden therein. Always try to take away with you the remembrance of any words or little sayings in the sermon which may have touched you; it would be well even to write them down. It is a very salutary practice for parents to question their children regarding the sermons which they have heard in order to know how much they have understood, and with what attention they have listened.

III. What does it mean "to bring forth fruit in patience"? It means to practise patiently and perseveringly what you have learned from the Word of God and to apply it to your daily life and work. Struggle, therefore, daily against your evil inclinations, against pride, anger, disobedience, and spiritual sloth. Live, not according to the corrupt principles of the world, but according to the Gospel and following the example of the saints; fervently implore of your divine Savior to strengthen you with His grace that you may overcome all temptations. Continual prayer, continual labor, continual struggling: such is the way to the kingdom of Heaven which ever "suffereth violence, and the violent bear it away."[1]

"He that hath ears to hear, let him hear," said

---
[1] Matt. xi, 12.

our Lord in concluding this parable. By these words He would point out the necessity and the importance of His teaching and urge you to follow it. Therefore, dear Brethren, hear the Word of God, believe and obey.

Look up and see the Blessed in Heaven, whilst on earth they listened to the Word of God, they practised it in their daily lives, and thus they attained eternal happiness. Then descend in spirit to the prison houses where countless lost souls shall weep and groan for all eternity. Indifference to the Word of God has brought them thither, for it is this which fills Hell.

Henceforth, treasure as your most valued possession the teachings of Jesus Christ; live according to them and strive to bring forth fruits worthy of salvation, that thus the divine Word may lead you to eternal happiness. Amen.

QUINQUAGESIMA SUNDAY
Luke xviii, 31–43
Healing of the Blind Man

> "Jesus, Son of David, have mercy on me."
> Luke xviii, 38.

Our holy Mother the Church, anxious for the spiritual welfare of her children, wishes us during this season of Lent to meditate more frequently on the bitter sufferings which the Son of God endured in order to atone for all the sinful pleasures in which men indulge, especially in so many places during the Carnival time.

By the reading of to-day's Gospel she would cure our spiritual blindness that we may not perish with a sinful world.

Let us consider the terrible misfortune of spiritual blindness and its cure by Jesus Christ.

I. SPIRITUAL BLINDNESS

1. Blind and poor! How terrible a misfortune! And yet how infinitely greater the misfortune, the unhappiness of those who are spiritually blind.

The man upon whom even the eternal truths make little or no impression, who is unmoved, either by the threat of hell-fire or the promise of heavenly happiness, who is indifferent to the beauty of virtue, who regards not the hideousness of vice: that man is spiritually blind. Such blind men as these heed not Jesus Crucified Who will one day be their Judge, nor do they ever regard the example of the Saints; they fall from one sin into another and they live as much at their ease as if there were no God, no eternal punishments.

This spiritual blindness is a punishment for sin, inflicted especially on those who live in the habitual state of sin. Their own malice has blinded them.[1]

A sick person who no longer feels anything is in a very serious state, and a person, spiritually blind, who no longer sees the light of Truth is indeed near to destruction.

2. Dear Brethren: If you would escape spiritual blindness, you must learn to know your predominant fault. There are many who have not this knowledge and they only accuse themselves of lesser faults. Judas considered himself blameless because he said that the precious ointment, instead of being poured out upon our divine Lord's sacred Feet, should have been sold, and the price given to the poor. But, avariciousness was the underlying motive which made him say this. It is the same with the proud, the sensual, the slothful, the unjust; they regard their vices as trifles.

Therefore, fight against your evil inclinations; avoid the occasions of sin; seek help in prayer, in the Sacraments and you will certainly escape spiritual blindness.

---

[1] Wisdom, ii, 21.

II. CURED BY JESUS CHRIST

1. The blind beggar in the Gospel called our divine Lord a son of David and, full of faith, besought His help, "Jesus son of David, have mercy on me." How wise of this blind man to profit by the presence of Jesus. If, from fear of men he had not availed himself of this opportunity, he would have lived and died in his blindness. In the same way there are precious moments in our lives when Jesus enlightens our souls with the light of His divine grace, these moments may never come again, it often happens that they never do. Well for the poor sinner who is faithful to grace, and with his whole heart calls to Jesus: "Jesus son of David, have mercy on me, a miserable blind man." Those who went before roughly rebuked the blind beggar in the Gospel and told him to be silent but he only cried the louder "Son of David, have mercy on me."

Never, dear Brethren, allow yourselves to be led away from our divine Lord by the jeers and mockery of others. Where Jesus is, there is joy of heart, there is salvation. Where He is not, there is unrest, unhappiness, never-ending despair.

Let us imitate this blind man in his gratitude. He made use of his eyes to gaze with wondering adoration upon his divine Benefactor, of his tongue to praise Him, of his feet to follow Him. We have indeed received a thousand benefits from God since childhood. Use your eyes in raising them to Heaven in prayer, your hands in labor for God, your feet in visiting Him in His Churches, your intellect in treasuring the lessons of Jesus Christ, your will in loving God above all things. Amen.

First Sunday in Lent

Matt. iv, 1–11

Temptations

> "Then Jesus was led by the Spirit into the desert, to be tempted by the devil."
> Matt. iv, 1.

Dear Brethren: In to-day's Gospel we read that the divine Spirit led our Lord into the desert that He might be tempted by Satan. It is all important for us to remember that God permits all men to be tempted for one or other of these reasons: Either we have grown tepid and careless in the fulfilment of the duties of our Religion thereby being deprived of spiritual consolation, or

God tries us as gold is tried in the furnace, to test our strength and if we are willing to serve Him without consolation. Finally, He allows us to be tempted in order to show us that of ourselves we are nothing; that we owe everything to God's grace, and therefore that we should pray for this divine grace very fervently. "Without me, you can do nothing," says Jesus Christ, and He places in our hands the weapon with which we shall be able to overcome the Enemy of our salvation; Prayer and fasting.

I. *Temptations to inordinate love of good things and pleasure:* "If thou be the Son of God, command that these stones be made bread."

How many sins are committed for the sake of the goods of this world, often, merely, for a home, a living. How many girls marry for riches; for position; fine clothes. And how often do do they bitterly repent their folly. What misery, even shame and disgrace too often result from the yielding to temptations of this nature. How many of such marriages result in life-long remorse and wretchedness.

II. *Temptations to Pride:* "If thou be the Son of God, cast thyself down, for it is written: 'That he hath given his angels charge over thee, that they keep thee, and in their hands shall they bear thee up, lest perhaps thou dash thy foot against a stone.'" "It is written again," said our divine Lord, 'Thou shalt not tempt the Lord thy God.'"

Beware, dear Brethren, of tempting God, especially, you, young people who are so apt to act without reflection. You tempt God when recklessly and without necessity you rush into danger, thereby running the risk of losing your life; when you frequent the company of those who may lead you into sin. Above all, avoid intercourse with those who have no faith, with unbelievers, with those who would teach you another faith, another code of morality than that taught by the Catholic Church.

III. *Temptations to Avarice:* "All these will I give thee, if falling down thou wilt adore me." But then our Lord answered: "Begone, Satan: for it is written *The Lord thy God shalt thou adore, and him only shalt thou serve.*"

Every sin is an act of idolatry, for by it, we reject the true God and prefer to Him Who is the eternal Source of all good, transitory riches, sinful pleasures, temporary gain. These things become, as it were, the sinner's idol which he sets up on the altar of his heart.

At our Lord's words, Satan fled, confounded, and many angels came and ministered to Jesus.

My Brethren, fight bravely against temptation; do not barter your eternal happiness, the ineffable joys of Heaven, for a moment of fleeting pleasure. If you have to fight against many temptations; if you have to bear much trouble, do not grow discouraged. Temptations are the furnace in which men's hearts are tried and purified; without temptation, there is no fight, without fighting, no victory, without victory, no crown.

"Blessed is the man that endureth temptation; for when he hath been proved, he shall receive the crown of life, which God hath promised to them that love him." [1] Amen.

Second Sunday of Lent

Matt. xvii, 1–9

The Transfiguration

> "This is my beloved Son, in whom I am well pleased: hear ye him." Matt. xvii, 5.

DEAR BRETHREN: The three disciples who were permitted to behold Jesus Christ in the splendor

---

[1] St. James, i, 12.

of His divinity on Mount Thabor were afterwards the witnesses of His awful agony in the Garden of Olives. If these disciples had not been previously strengthened by seeing the glory of their divine Master in His Transfiguration, how easily they might have been scandalised and have lost faith when they saw Him in His Agony. This glorious vision of the Transfiguration should also strengthen our faith and hope in Jesus. In order that we may be thus strengthened let us:

I. *Meditate on Heaven.*

II. *Hear Jesus Christ.*

I. MEDITATE ON HEAVEN

How immeasurably great must be the happiness of Heaven. The disciples tasted but a drop of this happiness; they saw but a few rays from the divine Face of Jesus, and yet they were so transported out of themselves with joy and ecstasy that they despised the society of men; they regarded as nought all earthly things, and wanted to remain for ever with their divine Master on Mount Thabor.

What unutterable rapture will fill our souls when, released by death, we shall behold the Beatific Vision and shall be immersed in the ocean of those heavenly joys which eye has not seen nor ear heard nor has it entered into the heart of man to conceive.

Oh! then, spare no effort, shrink from no labor, that by a good life you may merit to share in the glorious Vision of God. Could we but get one glimpse of the divine beauty of our Lord in Heaven, we should ever more cry out with the Apostle "I desire to be dissolved, and to be with Christ."[1] "Unhappy man that I am, who shall deliver me from the body of this death."[2] We read in the life of Saint Teresa that God permitted her to see a few rays of His divine Splendour. And ever afterwards all the joys of earth to her were but vain trifles, the loveliest beings in her eyes as shrivelled corpses; even the glittering stars and the silver moon seemed to her but gloomy shadows.

What joy then, my Brethren, shall be ours when one day we behold God no longer darkly as in a glass but face to face. Oh! let us often meditate on Heaven.

II. HEAR JESUS CHRIST

This is my beloved Son, Jesus Christ, says the Eternal Father "hear ye him." And in these words He points out to us the right road by which

---

[1] Phil. i, 23.   [2] Rom. vii, 26.

we shall reach Heaven, that is to say, if we would attain eternal happiness we must hear and follow the teaching of our divine Saviour.

Hear, therefore, and obey the precepts of Jesus Christ. For he is the Way, the Truth, and the Life and He will be our everlasting reward.

Hear Him and make use of the means of salvation which He offers you that you may attain to eternal bliss.

Hear Him when He says to you: Do penance, for the kingdom of Heaven is at hand. Through Him and His representatives alone can you obtain forgiveness of sins and peace of conscience. Hear Him when He invites you to partake of the most Holy Sacrament of the Altar. For he tells us in the plainest words. " I am the living bread which came down from heaven. If any man eat of this bread, he shall live forever." [1] Hear Him when He warns you not to let your heart be too much attached to the goods of this world, but rather to strive for the things of eternal life— for virtue and piety.

Hear Him when He tells you that you must love God above all things and your neighbor as yourself; when He exhorts you to endure trials and

---

[1] John vi, 51.

contradictions in patience unto the end, and never to murmur against the divine Will.

O most loving Jesus, be our Mediator with Thine Eternal Father at whose right hand Thou art seated that we may not be judged according to our sins, but that by our contrition and confession we may attain to Thy Glory which Thou hast purchased for us through Thy Sacred Passion and Death. Amen.

Third Sunday in Lent

Luke xi, 14–28

The Casting Out of a Dumb Devil

> "And he was casting out a devil, and the same was dumb:"
> Luke xi, 14.

Blessed are you, dear Brethren, as our divine Lord says in to-day's Gospel when you hear the word of God and follow it.

What does the Word of God tell us to-day? It tells us of the existence of the evil spirits; these form in themselves a kingdom, "the kingdom of Satan," which is utterly hostile and in eternal antagonism to the Kingdom of God. Idolatry and wickedness are the devil's works by which he seeks to lead men astray, to wrest them from God and to cheat them of eternal happiness. But the Son of God undertook to wage war against the prince of darkness, and the decisive combat took place on Calvary. The casting out of the evil spirits from those possessed by them by Jesus Christ during His life were but as so many skirmishes whereby the out-posts of Hell were partially destroyed.

Let yourselves also be healed, dear Brethren, through Jesus Christ.

I. SPIRITUAL DUMBNESS

The Evil one often makes the sinner dumb. In the first place, he renders him dumb with regard to God, in as much as he no longer prays nor begs pardon from the Lord for his sins, and he has a distaste for and an unwillingness to receive the Sacraments, and for every devotional practice.

Satan makes the sinner dumb with regard to his fellow men. For he is silent about the sins of others, many of which he could prevent and thus avert much temporal injury, but he does not do this, on the contrary, he listens to the most fearful blasphemies, to slanders and calumnies without ever uttering a protest.

Satan makes an habitual sinner dumb with regard to himself. For he causes him to feel great dislike and fear of confession, and even if the poor sinner does go to confession, alas! he often conceals his most grievous sin because of the shame with which the devil inspires him.

Saint Cyril once saw the devil standing at a confessional and asked him what he was doing there. He answered that he was giving back stolen goods, namely, the shame which he takes from man when he sins. Therefore always say to yourself before Confession: "In defiance of the Evil One and for love of my God Whom I have offended, I will confess my sins truthfully."

II. RELAPSE INTO SIN

Our divine Savior warned the Jews that they would relapse into the sin of unbelief, and would become completely hardened and impenitent.

Alas! this happens to many Christians. The first time a man sins, God freely forgives him, especially, if he has sinned through weakness or ignorance. But the oftener he relapses into the same sins the stronger will grow his passions, the more deliberate will be his sin, the more his malice, his indifference, his presumption will increase. Such is the lesson taught by sad experience.

The devil is called an unclean spirit because he tries, more than all, to tempt men to the sin of impurity. When once through lust and sensuality he becomes master of the human heart, it is very difficult to drive him out; he may indeed be driven many times out of an unclean heart, but he always finds ways and means to return, for the sinner is already by his own evil desires attracted to this sin; often, unfortunately, even those advanced in years are unable to overcome this vice. Hence, dear Brethren, beware of this sin to which men so easily become habituated, and which it is so difficult to overcome.

O Heavenly Father! we acknowledge that we are weak, erring creatures; help us with Thy grace that we may purify our hearts by penance, and that we may never again relapse into sin. We implore this grace through Thy divine Son, Jesus Christ. Amen.

Fourth Sunday in Lent
John vi, 1-15
Without God We Can Do Nothing

> "And Jesus took the loaves: and when he had given thanks, he distributed to them that were set down. In like manner also of the fishes, as much as they would."
> John vi, 11.

DEAR BRETHREN: A vast multitude numbering 5000 persons, not including women and children, had for three days crowded round our Lord, forgetful of all earthly cares and business as they listened to His teaching, so wholly absorbed therein that they heeded nothing else, intent upon the one thing which is, indeed, alone necessary. For to know what Jesus Christ teaches and to follow it should be the supreme concern of our lives.

As we read in to-day's Gospel, our divine Lord rewarded the people's fervor by the miracle of the multiplication of the loaves and fishes.

From this miracle we learn that equally as in spiritual matters success in temporal affairs depends upon God's blessing.

1. Without God we can achieve nothing in

temporal matters, although there are men who attribute all their success to their own brains, their own efforts, industry, skill, their own good luck. No: our divine Lord has said "without me you can do nothing"; consequently we can do absolutely nothing. Labor in your fields; manure; plough; weed; harrow. But unless God sends seasonable weather, unless He sends rain and sunshine at the right time, can you make the corn spring up and grow; can you, without God's blessing, cause even a single blade of grass to spring up? And when the crops are growing well, giving promise of a rich harvest, who wards off the thunder-storm, the hail which would blight all that fair promise? When God withholds His blessing, all our trouble, all our labor is vain and unprofitable; without His blessing we can have no earthly prosperity. As with the fruit of the earth so it is with all the affairs and undertakings of men.

Dear Brethren, What must you do to draw down upon you God's blessing? First of all, God wills that you should ask of Him His help and blessing: "Ask and it shall be given you: seek and you shall find: knock, and it shall be opened to you."

Pray especially during the Holy Sacrifice of the Mass, because then we have on the Altar as our Mediator with the Eternal Father Jesus Christ Himself. Keep Sunday holy, for thus you will obtain for yourself God's greatest blessings. Maintain good order in your home, especially amongst your children, lest, being ill-taught and badly brought up, they bring upon you a curse instead of a blessing. Watch over your servants; good, pious servants bring a blessing on the house.

But in the spiritual order of things, even more than in the temporal, all depends on God's blessing.

II

Without the grace of God no sinner can repent, can amend his life. "No man can come to me," says our Lord, "except the Father, who has sent me, draw him—"

Man has in himself evil inclinations which draw him to sin. If a sinner wishes to amend his life, he must conquer his evil inclinations of whatever nature they may be—to sensuality, to avarice, to sloth, to pride. He must detest the sin to which, hitherto, he has felt an attraction; he must give himself wholly to God's service. But, without help from Heaven, without the grace of God, he can never succeed in doing these things.

St. Augustine experienced this in himself. For a long time he was quite sensible of what a shameful life he was leading; he recognised the enormity of his guilt in yielding to his passions; he wished to amend his life, to avoid the occasions of sin. But he found himself unable to do so. What was wrong with him? He had not grace. God, indeed, pursued him with His grace, but St. Augustine fled from Him. When he received God's grace, then he found it easy to avoid sin, easy even to become a Saint.

Dear Brethren: This is a solemn truth. Implore of the all-merciful God that He may never deprive you of His divine grace, that He may at all times assist you to keep His Commandments. Thus will His blessings be ever upon you, both in your spiritual and temporal concerns, until we all enter into the Kingdom of everlasting happiness to be with our Lord Jesus Christ in His eternal glory. Amen.

Fifth Sunday of Lent

John viii, 46–59

The Sin of Impenitence

> "They took up stones therefore to cast at him. But Jesus hid himself, and went out of the temple." John viii, 59.

Dear Brethren: In to-day's Gospel Jesus Christ appears before us in all His divine Majesty. It was the last public effort of His love to win the people to believe in Him and thus secure their eternal salvation. But the attempt to stone Him which was their reply to these merciful efforts proved the hardened impenitence of the Jews.

O most loving Saviour! preserve us all from the awful sin of impenitence.

1. Let us first contemplate our Lord as He is presented to us in the Gospel. Calm, unmoved, in His divine majesty He stands in the midst of the angry crowd and asks that tremendous question. "Which of you shall convince me of sin?" Never before as long as the world had lasted, had anyone dared to utter such words, and of all the men who have ever dwelt on earth not one could proclaim himself without sin, as Jesus Christ has now done. He is the Model and

the Mirror of all holiness; His divine nature excluded all possibility of sin.

As man, His moral character was absolutely stainless. His doctrine was Truth itself; His miracles proved His Divinity; His virtues shone resplendent as the sun. When the Jews insulted Him with the vilest blasphemy, calling him a Samaritan (heretic), a devil, He proved His innocence by His unalterable calmness, patience and meekness, although with one word He could have struck them to the ground, as He did later the rabble in the Garden of Olives.

Dear Brethren: Let us learn from our divine Saviour; we who are so easily roused to anger, let us bear insults for the love of God in silence. Let us pardon our fellow-men that we may obtain pardon of our own sins.

The Scribes and the Pharisees and the people who were led astray by their leaders could not answer the divine Master, and in their rage they insulted and blasphemed Him, even going so as to stone Him.

There are still in these days proud bad men. The Truth we are told, begets hatred. Alas! for those whose souls are in a state of hardened impenitence, such souls are irreparably lost.

"They have eyes and see not. They have ears and hear not." [1]

Pharaoh saw with his own eyes how God through Moses worked the greatest miracles; he saw his country stricken with ten plagues, one after another, each one worse than that which had gone before. And yet he remained obdurate, until at last, the judgments of God overtook him and he perished in the Red Sea.

Here we see the prototype of those unhappy Christians who will not be converted by the greatest miracles or chastisements of God, those enemies of the Church who, the more gloriously God triumphs in His Church, the more enraged they become, those mockers of Religion who wilfully shut their eyes to the series of incontrovertible miracles by which for nineteen hundred years Christianity has been preserved. They cannot deny these truths, therefore, with blasphemies, with lies, with calumny they stone Christ, His Church and His servants.

But Christ withdraws from them. Once only shall they see Him again in the terrors of the Last Judgment when He will pronounce their sentence of eternal damnation.

---

[1] Ps. cxiii, 5–6.

Oh! dear Brethren, pray for these unhappy souls. And be, yourselves, faithful servants and followers of Jesus Christ that at the hour of your death He may appear to you with a gracious and favorable countenance. Amen.

Palm Sunday

Matt. 21, 1–9

> "Hosanna to the son of David: Blessed is he that cometh in the name of the Lord: Hosanna in the highest." Matt. xxi, 9.

Dear Brethren: To-day, in commemoration of our divine Lord's triumphal entrance into Jerusalem a few days before His Passion, the palm-branches which have been blessed by the priest are distributed to the Faithful who hold them in their hands during the procession which usually takes place on this day, when the priest, going outside the Church, knocks three times with the foot of the Cross at the door which is then opened. This ceremony signifies that the gates of Heaven which because of the sin of our first parents had been closed against us are now by the Passion and Death of our divine Saviour once more opened to us.

Let us contemplate Jesus Christ entering in triumph into the city of Jerusalem.

1. Why did our Lord who had hitherto lived such a hidden life in humble obscurity, shortly before His death make such a triumphal entrance into Jerusalem? He did so that the prophecy of Zacharias might be fulfilled. " Rejoice greatly, O daughter of Sion, shout for joy, O daughter of Jerusalem: BEHOLD THY KING will come to thee, the just and savior: he is poor, and riding upon an ass, and upon a colt the foal of an ass."[1]

When earthly kings return victorious from battle, they enter in triumphal procession into the capital of their kingdom. But all this glorious triumph has been won at the cost of fearful bloodshed and slaughter. Five days after His triumphant entry into Jerusalem Jesus would shed His Precious Blood for the salvation of His people. In His triumphal procession were no prisoners of war, no display of booty taken from the enemy. He entered Jerusalem to redeem His mortal enemies from the captivity of Hell, and then to reign by love, and to lead those who believe in Him, hope in Him, and love Him into the heavenly Jerusalem.

---
[1] Zach. ix, 9.

2. Dear Brethren: Jesus comes to us for this same end when we receive Him in our Easter Communion. He will reign in us and over us by His divine love, and if we are faithful to Him He will lead us into His Kingdom of everlasting happiness.

Oh! may we ever approach this most Holy Sacrament in which Jesus Christ, true God and true man, is really present, with the most profound reverence. Wo to those who like the Jews cry out. "We will not have this man to reign over us."[1] We prefer Barabbas, that is, we prefer sin, the gratification of our evil passions to Jesus Christ. How many are there who, even after they have received their divine Lord in Holy Communion, by their mode of life speak thus. What punishment awaits those guilty of such ingratitude? Surely the same which overtook the Jews to whom our Lord said, "For if you believe not that I am he, you shall die in your sin."[2] May God preserve you all from such a fate!

3. The people who took part in our Lord's triumphal procession, cried aloud in jubilation, "Hosanna to the son of David: Blessed is he that

---

[1] Luke xix, 14. [2] John viii, 24.

cometh in the name of the Lord: Hosanna in the highest." But our Lord knew that all these marks of honor, these praises, were prompted by the hope of earthly advantage. The Jewish people believed that He would free them from the Roman yoke. Five days later when they found themselves disappointed in their hopes, they cried out " crucify him." Oh! how poor a thing is the praise of men; how fickle is the human heart! There are many Christians who act like the Jews. Occasionally, when some great misfortune falls upon them, or, perhaps at Easter time, when they approach the Sacraments, they praise God, they adore Him. But very quickly they fall away from Him, and by violating His Commandments offer Him every possible insult.

Such Christians are as ungrateful as the Jews. Wo to those who, by their sinful lives, join in that awful outcry of the Pharisees: Away with Him, crucify Him. O divine Savior, grant us the grace never to relapse into our former sins. Strengthen us that we may persevere in loving and serving Thee until the end, that then with the elect in the heavenly Jerusalem, we may to all eternity, sing Thy divine praises. Amen.

EASTER

Easter Sunday

Mark xvi, 1–7

Easter Joy—Alleluia!

> "Be not affrighted; you seek Jesus of Nazareth, who was crucified: he is risen, he is not here, behold the place where they laid him."
>
> Mark xvi, 6.

DEAR BRETHREN: To-day let us celebrate joyfully the glorious Resurrection of our Lord Jesus Christ from the dead which is at once the seal and the supreme proof of the truth of His divine teaching. We believe, not in one who is dead, but in the Lord of Life who has said: "I am the resurrection and the life." [1]

Let us hasten with the pious women to the Sepulchre, and there with renewed faith and love let us declare our belief in our risen Savior.

---

[1] John xi, 25.

I. WHAT WERE THE PIOUS WOMEN DOING AT THE SEPULCHRE?

1. Mary Magdalen, Mary, the Mother of James, and Salome had purchased spices for the purpose of anointing the sacred Body of Jesus, and they went very early in the morning to the Sepulchre.

What a beautiful example, what a lesson for you, dear Brethren, in the devotion of these holy women. Do you go in the golden hours of morning, not indeed to the tomb, but to the Tabernacle where your living Savior waits for you that He may bless you? Oh! how precious is one Mass in which your Lord bestows on you His divine peace and blessing which will remain with you through all the cares and labors of the day. Imitate the example of the holy women at the Sepulchre by going, if possible, every day to early Mass. But, at least, never fail to consecrate each day to God by fervent morning prayer. Thus you will ensure His blessing on all your undertakings, and His protection in all the dangers to which we are continually exposed.

2. When they reached the Sepulchre and saw the great stone which closed the entrance, thus

preventing them from carrying out their intention of anointing our Lord's Body, the holy women asked one another in great dismay, "Who shall roll us back the stone from the door of the Sepulchre?"

God rewarded their piety by sending an angel to roll back the stone. But before this happened, our Lord had already risen from the dead. He, the God of all power, the Lord of life and death, had burst His bonds and passed through the stone which closed His tomb, as later He passed through the doors, which were shut, and stood in the midst of His disciples. To the holy women the great stone was an obstacle to the carrying out of their pious design of anointing the sacred Body of their divine Master. But for us sin is the great stone which prevents our free access to our Lord. Who then will roll away the huge stone of those evil habits which have clung to us so long? Such is the despairing cry of many a poor sinner. Ah! if you turn to God and with your whole heart call upon Him for help, to you also He will send an angel in the person of a priest who will absolve you from your sins, and restore divine peace to your soul.

II. THE ANGEL'S WORDS

" Fear not you; for I know that you seek Jesus who was crucified . . . going quickly, tell ye his disciples that he is risen: and behold he will go before you into Galilee; there you shall see him. Lo, I have foretold it to you."

Our divine Lord's Resurrection from the dead is the pledge that we too shall one day rise from the grave. As Jesus Christ in His glorified Body came forth from the tomb so also, the bodies of the just, more resplendent than the sun, shall rise from the grave, and united to their souls shall be able to transport themselves with the rapidity of thought whithersoever they will.

At our graves also on that day will stand an angel, our Guardian Angel, who will greet us as his brethren, now immortal like himself. Then, dear Brethren, fear shall be no more, for we shall be for ever with Jesus.

O Lord Jesus Christ! we rejoice that Thou hast risen from the dead victorious over Death and Hell, thereby reconciling us to God, and opening to us the gates of Heaven. Oh! draw us to Thee; help us to avoid sin and to serve

Thee faithfully, that thus after our glorious resurrection we may have eternal life. Amen.

Low Sunday

John xx, 19, 31

Our Lord's Easter Gift

> "Peace be to you."
> John xx, 19.

DEAR BRETHREN: In the liturgy of the Church, this, the first Sunday after Easter from the earliest ages has been called White Sunday. In the early ages of the Church the Sacrament of Baptism was administered on this day to those who desired to become Christians, the Catechumens as they were called. As a sign of the spotless purity of those souls now washed from every stain of sin in the cleansing waters of Baptism, the newly-baptised received white garments which they wore for eight days, putting them off on this Sunday, whence its name of White Sunday.

Happy are you, my Brethren, if you have preserved that beautiful robe of sanctifying grace which you received in Baptism. Clothed in this garment your soul shines before Heaven more resplendent than the sun. But, if some amongst you have been so unhappy as to lose this robe of baptismal innocence by sin, let them profit now by this Paschal time, by the love of their Heavenly Father, to regain sanctifying grace in the Sacrament of Penance. It is to this end that our Lord in to-day's Gospel by His divine salutation, offers to us His precious Easter gift, *"Peace be to you."*

1. Three times He speaks those words, "Peace be to you," to His disciples and also to us. Jesus Christ could bring us nothing better than peace. What contentment, what happiness fills our souls when we are at peace with God, with our conscience, with our neighbor. Therefore, make your peace with God Who pardons all who repent sincerely. Let nothing remain on your conscience which might trouble you on your death bed. As far as in you lies, live in harmony with everyone; rather, in obedience to our Lord's injunction suffer loss than become involved in strife with your neighbor. In this way, you will have peace here on earth and may hope for eternal happiness hereafter.

2. In order that we may all share in this most precious Easter gift, our divine Lord, on this

day, bestowed on His Apostles and through them on their successors, the bishops and priests of the Catholic Church, the power of remitting and retaining sins. "As the Father hath sent me, I also send you." And then after these words Jesus breathed upon His Apostles, saying "Receive ye the Holy Ghost. Whose sins you shall forgive, they are forgiven; and whose *sins* you shall retain, they are retained."

From these words it follows clearly that power was given to the Apostles and to their successors to remit the sins of all those who should with sincere repentance confess their sins. But, neither the Apostles nor their successors received power to forgive the sins of those who should refuse to fulfil this condition of contrite confession. What consolation we receive in this sacrament of Penance by which our souls are cleansed from even the greatest sins; our consciences are once more at rest, and we enjoy that heavenly peace without which we can find no happiness on earth.

Dear Brethren: never be ashamed of acknowledging your sins in confession; these sins are, indeed, in themselves, a cause of shame to us, **but, when** we confess them, firmly resolving never to commit them again, then we blot out our disgrace.

Conclusion. O Sweetest Jesus, we implore Thee through that incomprehensible love which led Thee to die for us upon the Cross, to visit us thy poor weak creatures, and to grant us that peace which the world cannot give: peace with God, with our neighbor, with our conscience, that thus we may happily complete our life's journey, and attain to the possession of that everlasting peace which Thou hast prepared for us in Thine eternal Kingdom. Amen.

Second Sunday after Easter
John x, 11-16

> "I am the good shepherd,
> "The good shepherd giveth his life for his sheep."
> John x, 11.

Dear Brethren: In the old Testament the Prophets had already made use of this beautiful image of the good shepherd when predicting the coming of our divine Redeemer. Speaking through the mouth of the Prophet Ezechiel,[1] God says of Himself, "I will feed my sheep— I will feed them in the most fruitful pastures—

---
[1] Ezech. xxxiv, 14-16.

I will seek that which was lost; and that which was driven away, I will bring again; and I will bind up that which was broken—and I will feed them in judgment." In to-day's Gospel, Jesus Christ makes use of the same most beautiful image, and describes Himself as the good Shepherd.

I. JESUS THE TRUE GOOD SHEPHERD

1. Well, indeed, may our Lord describe Himself as the good Shepherd, for He has given His life for His sheep, and still continues to watch over them. He has poured out upon them His divine Spirit, and has provided them with His appointed representatives who will lead them to His chosen pastures, that thus we who are His sheep may all attain to the eternal happiness which He has prepared for us in Heaven.

Very beautiful are the words of St. Ambrose. "Are you wounded, then is Jesus the physician who will heal your wounds. Are you burning with the fire of evil passions, then is He the spring whose cooling waters will quench thy thirst. Does the burthen of sin weigh you down, then is He the righteous One who will raise you up. Are you in need of help, then is He the power and the strength which will support you.

Do you fear death, then is He the life which will deliver you from eternal death. Do you long for Heaven, then is He the way which will lead you thither. Do you fear the darkness, then is He the light which will dissipate it. Do you need nourishment, then is Jesus the food which will nourish and strengthen you."

In all your necessities, therefore, have recourse, full of confidence, to our Lord who is the best of Shepherds.

"Who did no sin, neither was guile found in his mouth. Who his own self bore our sins in his body upon the tree; that we being dead to sins, should live to justice: by whose stripes you were healed. For you were as sheep going astray; but you are now converted to the shepherd and bishop of your souls." [1]

II. ARE WE HIS INDEED, HIS SHEEP

1. "*I know mine and mine know me.*" Ask yourself seriously: Do I indeed acknowledge Jesus Christ as my good Shepherd, my Savior, my Redeemer? If you desire to know Jesus better, you must be zealous in hearing the Word of God, in attending sermons.

---
[1] I Pet. ii, 22–25.

Jesus Christ is the eternal Son, the Word of the Father, by whom all things have been created, He is our Savior, and by means of His Sacraments He gives us the grace to become His children. In Heaven He still bears the marks of His Sacred Wounds, and is our constant Mediator with His Eternal Father. Therefore, in times of trouble and of temptation call upon your divine Redeemer: O Jesus! my good Shepherd, save me from the Evil One. Be to me a Jesus, and sanctify me.

2. My sheep "shall hear my voice." Our divine Lord ever discharges the duties of His office of good Shepherd.

It is the voice of this good Shepherd which we often hear in the silence, exhorting us to perform this or that good action, warning us to avoid the company of those who would lead us into sin. It is the voice of this Good Shepherd which we hear when the priest explains to us the Gospel, or in the confessional encourages us to amend our lives; it is the good Shepherd's voice which we hear when some true friend gives us salutary advice. How beautiful are the words of St. Augustine when he says:

"My mother exhorted me to lead a chaste life,

and kept me from bad company, but I despised her exhortations as being spoken by the voice of a woman. And yet it was the voice of the good shepherd who was seeking His lost sheep."

Dear Brethren: if you would know whether you are to be numbered amongst the flock of Jesus Christ, the true good Shepherd, you have only to ask yourself if you follow His teaching. For St. John tells us:[1]

"He who saith that he knoweth him, and keepeth not his commandments, is a liar, and the truth is not in him." O Most loving Jesus! Who art the true good Shepherd, and who wilt one day appear to separate Thy chosen sheep from those who do not belong to Thee or recognise Thee, grant that on that day I may be found on Thy right hand amongst Thine elect, and may enter with them into the heavenly Fold where there shall be but one Shepherd and one flock. Amen.

---

[1] I John ii, 4.

Third Sunday after Easter
John xvi, 16–22

Jesus at His Last Supper Consoles the Disciples

"Yet a little while."
John xvi, 16.

DEAR BRETHREN: Never yet has one about to die spoken such touching, such beautiful farewell words to his friends as did our Lord to His disciples at His last Supper. As a father taking leave of his children, He imparted to them His blessing, speaking to them many consoling words and earnestly enjoining upon them obedience to His last instructions. Let us try to take home to ourselves three of these, that we, also, may derive from them strength and consolation.

I. "A LITTLE WHILE, AND NOW YOU SHALL NOT SEE ME: AND AGAIN A LITTLE WHILE, AND YOU SHALL SEE ME: BECAUSE I GO TO THE FATHER."

According to the interpretation of Saint Augustine, these words have a two-fold meaning. After the Last Supper the disciples would not see the divine Master again until He had risen from the dead on the third day after His death. And again, on the day of His Ascension into Heaven He would vanish from their sight.

But when the days of their earthly pilgrimage had come to a happy end, then would they be with Him for ever in Heaven. What supreme joy and consolation for all the elect.

Even the longest life is short when compared with Eternity; in the sight of God, a thousand years is but as yesterday which is already past. How infinitesimally small is a drop of water compared with the vast ocean. But far smaller the number of our days on earth compared with the boundless ocean of Eternity. Young people look forward to the long years which they think are theirs. But death is much nearer to some of them than they think, and they will have to appear before the Judgment Seat of God, there to receive eternal reward or punishment. At the hour of death, all the sufferings we have endured will seem as nothing. What matters transitory suffering, if we attain eternal happiness.

How foolish are those who for a momentary pleasure plunge into eternal misery. How short-lived the pleasure, how endless the misery.

II. "I GO TO THE FATHER"

When our divine Lord speaks of His death, He calls it "going to the Father." Ignominious indeed was His death, but yet most blessed. This is the joyous idea which the friends of God should conceive of death. For death is, indeed, "going to the Father" after weary wanderings, a going forth from the prison-house of the body to the blessed Home of the Father, to eternal union with God.

"I desire to be dissolved and to be with Christ" cries out Saint Paul, and with him, Ignatius, Polycarp, Teresa, and so many other Saints. So too should we often sigh forth our longing desires—My soul longs for Thee, O my God. . . .

But the impious man cannot say when he comes to die "I go to the Father"—that Father Whom during life he has contemned, Whom he has refused to obey, electing to serve Satan rather than God. Oh! dear Brethren, hear the words of the Lord: "Walk whilst you have the light, that the darkness overtake you not."[1]

III. "YOUR SORROW SHALL BE TURNED INTO JOY"

When our Lord after His Resurrection appeared to His disciples, their hearts overflowed with joy, and even later when much sorrow came to them, they still were filled with gladness,

---
[1] John xii, 35.

for they had the assured hope, that after their brief sufferings, eternal happiness would be theirs.

The world can offer no joy to be compared with that which we experience in the service of Jesus Christ, in the exercise of Religion. Pure joy springs from the love of God, from the faithful following of Jesus, from resignation to God's will, from the love of our neighbor. These joys will accompany us to the grave, will dispel the fear of death, will remain with us until they are merged in the everlasting joys of Heaven.

If we love God with our whole hearts then shall our Lord's promise be fulfilled in us. "Your heart shall rejoice; and your joy no man shall take from you."

Oh! strive that those precious everlasting joys may be yours. Amen.

Fourth Sunday after Easter

The Patronage of St. Joseph

> "Can we find such another man, that is full of the spirit of God?" Gen. xli, 38.

DEAR BRETHREN: The sublime dignity of the office to which Saint Joseph was called as the protector, the guide and foster-father of the Son of God on earth, and the spouse of Mary has caused the Church to appoint a special Feast in his honor, under the title of the Patronage of Saint Joseph which we celebrated to-day.

Let each one amongst us on this day implore of Saint Joseph that he would, in the first place, take upon himself the care of our eternal salvation, that thus we may never lose the grace of God, or, if so unhappy as to lose it, that we may speedily regain and preserve it until the end of our lives. "What doth it profit a man if he gain the whole world, and suffer the loss of his own soul?"

Because he guarded the greatest treasures of Heaven and earth, Jesus and Mary, St. Joseph is called the Treasurer of divine grace. Grace consists in beginning well the Christian life, in persevering in virtue, and in closing this life with a holy death. Pray fervently to St. Joseph for the grace of a happy death.

Secondly, let us ask the protection of St. Joseph that we may fulfil with exactitude the duties of our state in life. Every Christian has received from God some special vocation, and on his fidelity to this vocation depends his future happiness, and even his temporal welfare. We must therefore, always labor diligently, we must never be ashamed to labor, and as Christians, following the example of Saint Joseph, we should always offer our labor to God, with the intention of pleasing Him; we should faithfully fulfil our duties to God, and earnestly strive to acquire virtue. St. Joseph is called in Holy Scripture, "A just man," because he possessed all virtues in a perfect degree. We should be content with our position and calling whatever they may be, like St. Joseph, who although he belonged to the Royal house of David, labored with his hands, in complete submission to the Will of God.

Finally, we should implore the protection of St. Joseph for our country. The holiest of ties bind us to the land in which we were born, our native land, and we can never be indifferent to its welfare; its joys, its sorrows are ours.

Pray, therefore, dear Brethren, to St. Joseph, that he may ever preserve the Faith in fullest vigor and strength in this land of ours. A nation is only strong in as much as it possesses faith.

In these days unbelief is daily spreading more and more. How many of our youth, alas! when they leave school, lose their faith. Therefore, pray to St. Joseph, invoke his protection for our young people, that the precious jewel of faith may be preserved to them.

The blessing of the Eternal Father and of the Holy Family, Jesus, Mary and Joseph, be upon you now and at the hour of your death. Amen.

Fifth Sunday after Easter
John xvi, 23–30
"Full" Joy in Prayer

> "Ask and you shall receive: that your joy may be full."
> John xvi, 24.

Dear Brethren: When our divine Lord wished to teach us a lesson of supreme importance, He began with the words: "Amen, amen, I say unto you." And so we find these words prefacing His instruction on Prayer in to-day's Gospel. Now, in order that this "full" joy in prayer may be ours, let us consider how we should pray.

I. WE MUST PRAY IN THE NAME OF JESUS

"Amen, amen, I say to you," says our Lord, "if you ask the Father anything in my name, he will give it you." To pray in the Name of Jesus, means that we ask through the merits of Jesus

Christ, for being sinful creatures we are unworthy of being heard. But our Lord actually offers to His eternal Father on our behalf the merits of His Life, Passion and Death. He "is always living to make intercession for us."[1]

The Church strictly observes our divine Lord's ordinance. She begins her prayers with the words: O God, the Father of Mercy, and ends, "through the merits of our Lord Jesus Christ." Hence, before we offer our petitions to our Heavenly Father, we should humble ourselves before Him, saying: " I am a sinful creature utterly unworthy that Thou should hear me. Therefore, I unite my prayer to the merits of Jesus Who is my Mediator and my Advocate with Thee, He will supply for all my want of devotion."

The Church also turns to the Blessed Mother of God, to the Saints and the Angels, imploring of them as the friends of God to make intercession for us.

II. OUR JOY SHALL BE "FULL" WHEN WE ASK FOR THE RIGHT THINGS

Our divine Savior reproaches His disciples with not having asked for anything in His Name,

---

[1] Heb. vii, 25.

"Hitherto you have not asked any thing in my name."

Ah! how many amongst us are deserving of this reproach!

Sinners, you have not asked Jesus for "anything," because you have not yet prayed that He would give you the grace of repentance. Worldings, you who are wholly absorbed in the riches, the pleasures, the vanities of this world, you have not asked "anything" of God, for you have never implored of Him the love of virtue.

How many ask the Heavenly Father to give them a stone, that is to say, some temporal advantage which may lead them to eternal destruction?

2. What then are the things for which we should ask "that our joy may be full"? We should ask that we may be filled with an ardent desire of hearing and reading the Word of God whereby we may attain to a greater knowledge of God. For the greater our knowledge of God, the greater will be our love of Him. We should ask forgiveness for our sins, for sincere amendment of our lives, for the divine assistance in all temptations, and particularly, for the grace of final Persever-

ance; only those who persevere unto the end shall be saved.

We may, and indeed should, ask God for temporal favors, for health, for good weather, for a bountiful harvest; we may ask His blessing on our labors, our business, for relief in physical suffering, but when we ask for temporal favors we should always add those words of our Lord in His agony in the Garden of Gethsemane, "My Father, not as I will, but as thou wilt."

In the Our Father, Jesus Christ Himself teaches us that we should first ask for all that concerns the glory and honor of God, and then for what is needful to ourselves and our neighbor.

Now, dear Brethren, let the words of our divine Redeemer sink deeply into your hearts; let it be your constant endeavor to practise what He so earnestly enjoins. "Ask, and you shall receive; that your joy may be full. Watch ye, and pray that ye enter not into temptation." "Watch ye, therefore, praying at all times."

In the early morning pray that you may have strength to overcome the enemies of your salvation and may have God's blessing on your work; during the day often make short aspirations, little acts of love: Lord, may I die rather than not love you. At night, pray; ask forgiveness for your faults, and commit yourself to the protection of the Sacred Heart of Jesus that resting in Him you may enjoy the blessing of sound, refreshing sleep.

Dear Brethren, he who prays well, lives holily, and he who lives holily will die a happy death and enjoy God for all eternity. O Lord Jesus Christ! teach us how to pray. Amen.

Sixth Sunday after Easter

John xv, 26–27 and xvi, 1–4

Come, Holy Ghost!

> "The Spirit of truth, who proceedeth from the Father, he shall give testimony of me." John xv, 26.

Dear Brethren: In to-day's Gospel, our Lord promises that He will send upon us the divine Spirit. Let us, therefore, pray constantly that we may obtain this great grace.

"Come, Holy Ghost, fill the hearts of Thy Faithful and kindle in them the fire of Thy divine love."

What does the coming of this divine Spirit, the Holy Ghost, mean for us all?

I. THE HOLY GHOST IS THE GOD OF ALL CONSOLATION

Our Lord describes the Holy Ghost as the God of all consolation, for He will give to the disciples in contradictions and violent temptations comfort and fortitude. This promise has been fulfilled to the letter, for when the Jewish Sanhedrim ordered the Apostles to be scourged, and forbade them to preach in the Name of Jesus Christ, they went forth rejoicing that they were found worthy to suffer outrage for the Name of Jesus.

We learn from daily experience that life is filled with care and sorrow, and that but seldom amongst our fellow-men do we find true sympathy. Hence, in the tribulations which press so heavily upon us, we have indeed good reason to take refuge in the Holy Ghost Who will sweeten for us the bitterness of our suffering, and instead of the perishable goods of this world, will bestow upon us His divine grace which often fills our souls, even whilst still on earth, with greater joy than all the riches and pleasures of the world could give us.

II. THE HOLY GHOST IS A TEACHER OF TRUTH

"But when he, the Spirit of truth, is come, he will teach you all truth."[1]

"And I will ask the Father, that he may abide with you for ever."[2] Thus, this promise was given not only to the Apostles, but to their successors also.

Dear Brethren, be zealous in attending sermons wherein you will hear the doctrines of Christ, and strive to profit by them. What Jesus Christ Himself taught, the Holy Spirit still teaches us through the priests of the Catholic Church; whosoever obeys these, obeys the Holy Ghost; whosoever grieves these, grieves the Holy Ghost. Therefore "grieve not the holy Spirit of God."[3]

But, now comes the important question: How shall we prepare ourselves for the coming of the divine Spirit? Here we have for our guidance the example of our Lady and the Apostles and disciples.

1. They withdrew from the turmoil of the world, and for ten days remained in solitude and fervent prayer. If you would also receive the Holy Ghost, retire occasionally from the world and

---

[1] John xvi, 13.   [2] John xiv, 16.   [3] Eph. iv, 30.

hold converse with God. In the midst of continual distractions God's voice is not heard, but in solitude He speaks to the heart.[1] When it is not possible thus to withdraw from the world, at least, avoid unnecessary talk; close your eyes and ears to things that distract, and even when alone, be recollected and modest in your demeanor.

2. Purify your soul from the leaven of sin by contrite confession, and be reconciled to your neighbor, for the Holy Ghost only dwells in pure and peaceful souls.[2]

3. Until Pentecost let no day pass without praying most fervently that you may receive the seven gifts of the Holy Ghost, so that by Wisdom, Counsel, and Fortitude you may fight against all the enemies of your salvation, and at the end of life attain victory. Amen.

---

[1] Osee ii, 14.   [2] Ps. lxxv, 3.

PENTECOST

WHIT SUNDAY

John xiv, 23–31

The Gifts of the Holy Ghost

> "The fear of the Lord is the Beginning of wisdom."
> Ps. cx, 10.

DEAR BRETHREN: The Jews celebrated the great Feast of Pentecost in commemoration of the giving of the Law on Mount Sinai, and to offer to the Lord the first fruits of the earth. On the fiftieth day after His Resurrection, Jesus Christ, the Law-giver of the New Covenant, sent, as He had promised, the Holy Ghost upon His disciples who on that day publicly proclaimed the new Law of the Christian Religion, the Religion of Jesus Christ. Oh! dear Brethren, let us ever cherish an ardent devotion to the Holy Ghost without Whom we cannot even will to do good, far less accomplish it. To-day let us take for consideration two of the gifts of the Holy Ghost: Wisdom and the Fear of the Lord.

I. THE GIFT OF WISDOM

1. *Wisdom is the first gift of the divine Spirit.* This gift was given to the Apostles when the Holy Ghost descended upon them in fiery tongues, and they began at once to speak in various languages, so that they were understood by a multitude of people assembled from many lands and speaking different languages.

This gift of Wisdom enables man to recognise the end for which he has been created and the vanity of all earthly things; this gift chosen by King Solomon in preference to all others, enabled him to perceive that this world's honors, riches, pleasures quickly pass away, that they cannot satisfy the heart of man, that they leave behind them nothing but vexation of spirit, that only in loving and serving God can true happiness be found.[1] Later, this King, once so wise, gave himself up to the indulgence of his passions and the enjoyment of all sensual pleasures, but when he had sated himself with every earthly enjoyment, he was more dissatisfied than ever. He acknowledged that "The eye is not filled with seeing, neither is the ear filled with hearing."

---
[1] Eccles. 1.

O Holy Spirit! descend upon us with this gift of Wisdom, and fill our hearts with thy divine love, "For Wisdom will not enter into a malicious soul, nor dwell in a body subject to sins."[1]

II. THE GIFT OF THE FEAR OF THE LORD

Let us always pray, dear Brethren, for the Spirit of the Fear of the Lord. This Gift causes us to dread mortal sin as the greatest possible evil which could befall us, because by it we lose God's friendship and draw down upon ourselves temporal and eternal misery. We sometimes hear bad men saying, in a mocking voice, "I have sinned but what injury has it done me?" "Say not," says the Scripture, "I have sinned, and what harm hath befallen me? for the most High is a patient rewarder . . . . Delay not to be converted to the Lord, and defer it not from day to day, for His wrath shall come on a sudden, and in the time of vengeance, he will destroy thee."[2]

The fear of the Lord which is the gift of the Holy Ghost is not a slavish fear; it is a filial fear which causes us to dread offending our loving Heavenly Father; it is a fear for which we should always pray.

---

[1] Wisdom 1. [2] Eccles. v, 4–9.

"Pierce thou my flesh with thy fear:" cries out the Psalmist, "for I am afraid of thy judgments." [1]

Dear Brethren: strive earnestly, perseveringly, to avoid sin, but, if ever you should have the misfortune to offend God, then go without delay to seek His forgiveness in the Sacrament of Penance by a sincere, contrite confession. Thus, when death draws near, you will not fear his approach, for Satan, the prince of this world, will not be able to convict you of sin. Amen.

First Sunday after Pentecost
FEAST OF THE MOST HOLY TRINITY
Matt. xxviii, 18–20

The Baptismal Vows

> ". . . baptising them in the name of the Father, and of the Son, and of the Holy Ghost." Matt. xxviii, 19.

Dear Brethren: To-day's Gospel contains the last words spoken by our divine Lord to His disciples before His Ascension into Heaven, and it reminds us of the great grace which we received in our baptismal vows, "Going there-

---
[1] Ps. cxviii, 20.

fore, teach ye all nations; baptising them in the name of the Father, and of the Son, and of the Holy Ghost."

When we received the Sacrament of Baptism, we entered into a solemn covenant with Jesus Christ.

I. WHAT ARE THE OBLIGATIONS TOWARDS JESUS CHRIST WHICH WE HAVE CONTRACTED IN THIS BAPTISMAL COVENANT?

1. *To believe with firm unwavering faith in the teaching of the Catholic Church*, that is to say, in the teachings of Jesus Christ Himself. We believe in Christ. Unless we believe, Baptism will avail us nothing, save to brand us to all eternity in Hell. For is it written: " He that believeth and is baptised shall be saved: but he that believeth not shall be condemned." [1] Further we have promised:

2. *To Avoid Sin*. We renounced Satan and his works wholly and entirely. The works of Satan is sin. " He that committed sin," says St. John, "is of the devil." [2] In this promise to avoid sin is also included the promise to fly from the occasions of sin. For in vain do we resolve not to sin if we heedlessly expose our-

---
[1] Mark xvi, 16.   [2] I John iii, 8.

selves to the danger of sinning. Therefore, in Baptism we not only renounce Satan's works but also his pomps, those vain pleasures and amusements of which the Arch-enemy of man makes use to ensnare him; those perishable riches of this world with the deceitful glitter of which he fascinates so many and allures them from God. "If any man love the world, the charity of the Father is not in him."[1] Therefore, in the Covenant entered into in Baptism, we pledged ourselves to eternal enmity to Satan and to sin, and also to the world estranged from God, that world which is Satan's hireling, and which by its deceit and falsehood robs men of Heaven's everlasting riches. Finally we promise:

3. *To Lead a Virtuous Life.* "If thou wilt enter into life keep the Commandments." That is the first solemn admonition addressed to us in Baptism. We must put off the old man and put on the new who is modeled and formed according to Christ.

II. WHAT DOES CHRIST PROMISE US IN BAPTISM?

Dear Brethren: God's promises are far greater and more comprehensive than ours. He Who

---

[1] Ibid., I John ii, 15.

will never be outdone in generosity, in Baptism promises us:

1. *Remission of Original Sin and All Other Sins.* St. Peter in his instructions to the first Christians says:[1] "Do penance, and be baptised every one of you in the name of Jesus for the remission of your sins." And Saint Paul writing to the Ephesians says that "Christ loved the Church" as His Bride sanctifying and cleansing it "by the laver of water in the word of life . . . that it should be holy and without blemish."[2]

2. *Baptism, as the Council of Trent Declares,*[3] *also Remits All Temporal and Eternal Punishment Due to Sin.* "Those baptised are pure, stainless, sinless, so that there is nothing to prevent their immediate entrance into Heaven."

3. Baptism communicates to us sanctifying grace together with divine virtue, so that man receives a higher life, spiritual, heavenly, which is destined to last for ever.

4. *Baptism Stamps Our Souls with an Indelible Mark, and Makes Us Members of Christ and of His Church.* "For as many of you as have been baptised in Christ, have put on Christ."[4]

---

[1] Acts, ii, 38.
[2] Eph. v, 26, 27.
[3] Less, 5, Can 5.
[4] Gal. iii, 27.

Oh! dear Brethren, such are the great treasures and graces which the Son of God has bestowed on us in Baptism. Never forget your baptismal vows. Often recall them to mind. Renew them to-day on this Feast of the Holy Trinity; renew them on the anniversary of your First Communion, of your birth, on all Sundays and Festivals; in times of temptation renew them that you may not fall and break the oath of allegiance to Jesus Christ your King which you have taken.

Thus you will preserve unstained your baptismal innocence, and so when the time comes you will go before the Judgment Seat of Jesus Christ with confidence, before Him whom you have faithfully and perseveringly served, for Whose honor you have fought bravely, and Who in return will reward you with Eternal Life. Amen.

Second Sunday after Pentecost

The Great Supper

Luke xiv, 16–24

> "A certain man made a great supper, and invited many."
> Luke xiv, 16.

DEAR BRETHREN: This beautiful parable so rich in lessons for us, was proposed by our divine

Savior at a banquet to which He had been invited by a wealthy Pharisee.

In what ever surroundings our Lord found Himself, even at table, it was ever His wont to turn the thoughts of those around Him to spiritual things. From every circumstance of life He drew lessons and examples for the instruction and edification of the people.

According to the interpretations of the Fathers of the Church, in this Great Supper we are to recognise an image of the Church, of Eternal happiness, and also of the Most Holy Sacrament of the Altar.

THE KINGDOM OF CHRIST

It is God Himself who calls all men to believe in Jesus Christ and through this belief in Him wills that they should attain eternal happiness. Therefore, dear Brethren, in all the sufferings and trials of this life ever remember that the sufferings of the present time are not worthy to be compared with the glory to come.[1] Who would not bear patiently for one quarter of an hour, trials and sufferings, if thereby he could secure a thousand years of heavenly joys and happiness.

---

[1] Rom. viii, 18.

And our present troubles which compared with eternal happiness are but transitory and trifling, obtain for us, not merely a thousand years of happiness but, as St. Paul tells us "worketh for us above measure exceedingly an eternal weight of glory." [1]

The days of our mortal life are short, and the hour of the Great Supper will, for each and every one of us, soon strike. Sooner than we think, we shall hear the summons: "Come, gather yourselves together to the great supper of God:" [2]

Oh! what happiness shall be yours if in that hour, you are numbered amongst the Just.

THE MOST HOLY SACRAMENT OF THE ALTAR

The parable in to-day's Gospel may also be applied to that Banquet to which our divine Savior invites all His faithful followers, even were they as poor and despised as Lazarus.

In this Banquet Christ gives us Himself, His Flesh and Blood, as food, that we may have everlasting life.[3] He sends forth His priests to invite the Faithful to adore the most Holy Sacrament of the Altar and to exhort them to the more frequent reception of Holy Communion.

---

[1] II Cor. iv, 77.   [2] Apoc. xix, 17.   [3] John vi.

Let us prostrate ourselves before the Throne of the Lamb of God, praying "Thou art worthy, O Lord our God, to receive glory and honor and power:"[1] or with the centurion in the Gospel, "Lord, I am not worthy that Thou shouldst enter under my roof; say but the word and my soul shall be healed."

Our divine Savior Himself, calls us "Come to me all ye that labor and are heavy burdened, and I will refresh you."[2] Dear Brethren, go very often to our Lord Who for love of you, remains hidden night and day in the Tabernacle. Come, let us adore Him; let us prostrate ourselves before Him. For He it is Who has created us; He is our God and our Lord. Be present therefore, as often as you can at the Adorable Sacrifice of the Mass. But, if during the week, you are prevented by your occupations from hearing daily Mass, then each morning, unite your prayers with the Sacrifice offered by the priest on the Altar; thus each day you will receive many graces for the sanctification of your immortal soul, and our Lord will say to you those same words which at His Last Supper He spoke to His disciples. "And I dispose to

---

[1] Apoc. iv, 11. [2] Matt. xi, 28.

you a kingdom that you may eat and drink at my table, in my kingdom."[1]

THIRD SUNDAY AFTER PENTECOST

Luke xv, 1–10

Feast of the Sacred Heart

> "Rejoice with me, because I have found my sheep that was lost." Luke xv, 6.

DEAR BRETHREN: To-day's Gospel contains for us a message of joy, a message of consolation for all sinners, and thus is perfectly suitable to the great Feast of the Sacred Heart of Jesus which we celebrate. Our divine Savior in this parable of the lost sheep seeks to make us understand how willingly God pardons His sinful creatures, if we only try to amend our lives. He seeks to make us understand that God wills not the death of a sinner, but rather that he be converted and live.

Listen to the voice of the good Shepherd. "What man of you that hath an hundred sheep: and if he shall lose one of them, doth he not leave the ninety-nine in the desert, and go after that which was lost until he find it? And when

---

[1] Luke xxii, 29–30.

he hath found it, lay it upon his shoulders rejoicing: And coming home call together his friends and neighbors, saying to them: Rejoice with me, because I have found my sheep that was lost. I say to you, that even so there shall be joy in heaven upon one sinner that doth penance, more than upon ninety-nine just who need not penance."

Now, dear Brethren, the divine Heart of this good Shepherd is with us in the Adorable Sacrament of the Altar, and is our sweetest resting-place.

OUR SWEETEST RESTING-PLACE

As our divine Redeemer hung upon the Cross, one of the soldiers opened His sacred Side with a lance.[1] Wherefore? Dear Brethren, that in the divine Heart of Jesus, we, with all our sins, all our good works, all our love, as with all our sorrows, might find a secure refuge.

Does the burden of your sins press all too heavily upon you, and does it seem to you that your sins are too great and too many for you to hope that God would forgive you? Oh! then, take refuge in the Sacred wounded Heart

---

[1] John xix, 34.

of Jesus; listen to those words: "Behold this Heart which has so loved men and which for your sake has been wounded, cast all your sins therein, with my heart's blood will I wash them away." Commit to this Sacred wounded Heart all your good works, few, indeed, though these may be, yet, because they have been done for love of Him, your divine Saviour will turn them in precious jewels to be kept in His Sacred Heart until the dawn of that day when you shall receive your eternal reward.

Love the wounded Heart of Jesus with all the love of your heart. Ever will that heart of yours be restless, unhappy, until with its entire love it finds rest, rest here on earth and eternally in Heaven, in the Heart of Jesus.

Place all your sufferings, your sorrows, also, in the wounded Heart of your Redeemer. No matter how great, how bitter your sorrows, your sufferings may have been, or perhaps, are, even at this moment, remember that Jesus suffered them all before you, that for your sake, for love of you, He suffered inexpressibly more than you have suffered or could ever suffer. Should you then murmur or complain? Cast all your griefs into the divine Heart of Jesus and their bitterness will be changed into sweetness.

O Jesus! I choose as my abiding place Thy Sacred Heart, I come to Thee; ever more will I dwell with Thee, to love Thee more and more shall be my constant aim. Amen.

Fourth Sunday after Pentecost

Luke v, 1-11

All for Jesus

> "Master, we have laboured all the night, and have taken nothing; but at thy word I will let down the net."
>
> Luke v, 5.

DEAR BRETHREN: If in a time of great famine, a cart laden with bread were driven through some densely populated neighborhood, the poor people would gather in crowds that they might receive a portion of it, no matter how small. We should have the same great desire, the same hunger for the word of God which is the food and the nourishment for our souls that they may have eternal life. This is the lesson which we learn from those multitudes who, as we read in to-day's Gospel, pressed so closely round our Lord on the shore of the Lake of Galilee that He was obliged to take refuge on board a fishing vessel.

We also learn from Saint Peter how we should perform all our actions in the Name of Jesus and so bring down upon ourselves God's blessing.

"MASTER AT THY WORD"

What a beautiful example does Saint Peter give us!

1. *Peter was a Patient Laborer.* Although throughout the whole night he had endured cold and wet and want of sleep, yet no one heard him utter the least angry, impatient word though he had not taken one small fish.

You do yourself a great injury, if when your work is a failure, you get angry and curse. For you only make your work more difficult, a greater toil, you deprive yourself of the divine assistance and of the merit which that work might have gained for you in Heaven.

2. Peter was kind, generous, a faithful follower of Christ. He gave up his fishing vessel to His divine Master that He might preach to the people from the deck, whilst he himself with his companions listened attentively to the Master's discourse. He did not say, like so many who are

unwilling to help others: I want my ship myself, or I must go home now to dry my clothes. If he had acted in this unkind, ungenerous manner, he would not have got the great draught of fish, nor would he have become a disciple of Jesus.

Dear Brethren, you are mistaken and greatly deceived when you think that your work will suffer if you take time to say your morning prayers, or to assist at Mass.

Rather, be well assured that you labor in vain, that you watch and toil in vain, unless God makes your toil to prosper. For all depends on God's blessing.

3. *Peter was a laborer filled with faith and trust in the power and goodness of Jesus*, for he cast the net in the Name of Jesus. In effect, his words were: Dear Master, I know well from experience that night is the best time for fishing; surely, I shall have no better luck in the day-time, but at your command, I shall begin to fish again.

Brethren, whenever you are about to undertake some work, form your good intention and say like Peter, "At Thy word, O Lord! with Thy assistance, with Thy blessing, will I begin and carry out this work." If you often renew your good intention you will avoid the cursing so prevalent amongst workmen, and you will also surely refrain from all obscene language. Moreover, by your good intention you lay up for yourself golden treasures of merit, and thus the most trifling daily actions will one day procure for you greater happiness than if you had owned the riches of the whole world.

How beautiful the words of the wise Man. "The blessing of the Lord maketh men rich; neither shall affliction be joined to them."[1] Amen.

Fifth Sunday after Pentecost

Matt. v, 20-24

Woe to Him That Curses

> "And whosoever shall say, Thou fool, shall be in danger of hell fire." Matt. v, 22.

Dear Brethren: Let us, to-day, implore our divine Savior that He would give to each one of us a meek and humble heart, a heart ever ready to forgive, that so, we may be ever on our guard not to offend others, and that we may be always pre-

---
[1] Prov. x, 22.

pared to make peace with those who are hostile to us. For our Lord threatens the passionate with Hell, whilst to the peace-makers He promises Heaven.

TO THE PASSIONATE; HELL

The Pharisees, indeed, believed that murder was a great sin, but they made light of angry, malicious, revengeful feelings and of coarse abuse and insults. In the present day, also, there are many Christians who say: I am not a murderer nor a calumniator nor a thief. What is there to keep me out of Heaven?

You think that virtue consists in the mere avoidance of great sins and the doing of some few isolated good works. Our Lord has strictly forbidden us to give way to unjust anger, and He forbids us also to indulge in the desire of revenge, or the wish to injure our neighbor. He has placed anger, hate, and maliciousness on a par with murder. A man who gives way to rage is often the cause of more misery than a murderer. "Whosoever hateth his brother is a murderer," says St. John.[1]

Amongst the Jews the word "Fool" signified

---

[1] John iii, 15.

the greatest villain, one accursed of God. He who applies such terms to his fellow-man is guilty of hell-fire.

Dear Brethren, take our divine Lord's words, I implore of you, seriously to heart, He threatens those who curse and blaspheme with hell-fire, that fire which shall never be extinguished and in which sinners shall burn eternally.

Alas! how often do we hear Christians cursing one another, invoking every evil, even damnation, upon one another. How often do men call upon the devil to blast their fellow-men with temporal and eternal ruin. Yes: in their mad rage, they even invoke the holiest names in malediction upon those who have offended them. How often do husbands and wives, parents, brothers and sisters abuse one another, call one another by opprobrious names.

Ah! dear Brethren, with what horror should we regard such cursing, such abusive language. For when used with full deliberation, when habitually indulged in, it is a grievous sin.

BLESSED ARE THE PEACEMAKERS

Let us ever bear in mind the beautiful words of our divine Lord recorded in to-day's Gospel,

"If therefore thou offer thy gift at the altar, and there thou remember that thy brother hath anything against thee; Leave there thy offering before the altar, and go first to be reconciled to thy brother: and then coming thou shalt offer thy gift."

How can you refuse to be reconciled to your fellow-man, to seek his friendship, when this reconciliation is the condition on which God will pardon you your offenses and receive you into His divine Friendship? Therefore, when you have offended any man, seek as quickly as possible to be reconciled to him. Even if you have right on your side, do not continue at enmity; you must not let the sun go down upon your anger. Do not retire to rest until you have been reconciled with your friend.

O divine Jesus, who on the Cross didst pardon thine enemies and didst ask forgiveness for them from Thy Heavenly Father, grant us Thy grace that we too may ever pray for those who calumniate and persecute us, and so obtain Thy mercy and forgiveness for ourselves. Amen.

Sixth Sunday after Pentecost

Mark viii, 1–9

Multiplication of the Loaves and Fishes

> "And they did eat and were filled." Mark viii, 8.

DEAR BRETHREN: In to-day's Gospel, our divine Lord reveals Himself to us as a father providing his children with bread. With seven loaves and a few little fishes He satisfied the hunger of a crowd of people, numbering four thousand, the women and children not included. How much should this tender thoughtfulness for the hungry people encourage our confidence in the power and goodness of Jesus.

It is thus that He feeds us with the fruits of the earth which even now are ripening for our use. He satisfies our souls in Holy Communion with the Bread of Heaven.

In this miraculous multiplication of the loaves a great truth is conveyed to us.

I. God from little things can produce great results—Trust to His Mercy.

II. But He can also reduce great things to nought—Fear His Justice.

GREAT RESULTS FROM LITTLE THINGS

1. Almighty God shows us this in the Creation, for at His word alone, there came forth out of nothing the heavens and the earth, the sun, moon, stars and all living things, including Man: such a vast creation from one word. Surely we may say that here are great results from little things.

2. God shows us this truth also in the kingdom of Nature, in the harvest, in the fruits of the earth; you sow seed in the earth and from it there springs the corn, yielding a hundred fold of fruit.

3. This truth is shown to us amongst men, amongst nations. Joseph sold into Egypt as a slave, thrown into prison, through God's Providence became the Viceroy of the whole land. The small nation of Israel grew and increased until its numbers were as the sands of the seashore. Many a poor family by God's assistance and their own honesty and upright conduct have attained to great prosperity.

Dear Brethren, always trust to God's Almighty power and goodness, and you will not grow discouraged and despondent when you find that your means are insufficient. God can when He will, make the little you have grow into much more; He can also bless the little that you have, so that it will do far more for you than if you had a great deal more.

Real happiness does not depend on the amount of worldly goods you possess, but on the good use of what you have. The man who leads a virtuous life and is content, even though he have but little, has a fortune in that little, and is more satisfied with his frugal fare than the miser who with all his money is never satisfied. And remember, that in the hour of your greatest need God's help is nearest to you. For all things work to the good of those whom God loves.

GREAT THINGS REDUCED TO NOUGHT

But God can also bring great things to nought. Because men had become wicked and had given themselves up to their passions, in punishment for their sins, God sent the Deluge in which every living thing perished; of all the millions of men on earth, only eight were saved.

How often do we see men with large possessions in land whose fields and orchards promise a rich harvest; they have large herds of cattle. But bad weather, too much rain, hail, thunderstorms destroy the crops, blight the fruit-trees; disease attacks the cattle. How quickly does a man's prosperity vanish.

3. In families and individuals how often do we see the effects of God's chastisements on those who contemn His laws. How often do we see those who began life in good circumstances reduced to beggary because of their sins.

The whole history of the world proves that God's blessing is ever on those who serve Him in virtue and piety. On the contrary, all those who offended God by their sins and thus merited punishment from His justice, found no favor in His sight, and were overtaken by misfortune. For God often punishes sin here on earth as well as in Eternity. Experience teaches us that generally speaking, all good fortune, all blessing departs from the house whose inmates live in sin.

Dear Brethren, serve your God in true love and piety, and then He will bless you with the spirit of contentment, and thus though you may have but little, He will make that little great. But if you offend God by sin, His justice will require your punishment, and He will bring all that you have to nothing, He will withdraw His blessing from your home, and want and misery shall enter therein. May the blessing of God be with you always. Amen.

Seventh Sunday after Pentecost

Matt. vii, 15-21

False Prophets

> "Wherefore by their fruits you shall know them."
> Matt. vii, 16.

DEAR BRETHREN: Broad is the way which leads to destruction and many there are who enter upon it. But the gate into eternal life is strait and the way is narrow and few find it. These words were spoken by our divine Savior in His sermon on the Mount to His disciples and the multitudes gathered round Him. That we may not miss the right way, He warns us to-day to beware of evil leaders, of sinful men, of false prophets, such as were the Pharisees. "By their fruits you shall know them" said our Lord. These words apply to the present time also.

WHAT ARE THE BAD FRUITS?

The bad fruits are the teachings of unbelievers, the false doctrines of heretics; they are the seductive temptations to vice and a godless life arising from the example of others. When you hear anyone indulging in licentious language, jeering at Religion and devout practices; when he calumniates the priesthood; when he derides divine truths and the most sacred doctrines of the Catholic Church; when he scoffs at the Sacraments: then you may know that such a one is like the thistles and the thorns from which no good fruit, no grapes can be gathered.

My Brethren, I implore you to fly, as from the plague, from such men who would wrest from you your faith, your good conscience, your purity, who would deprive you of God's grace, who would plunge you into sin, and thus drag you to temporal and eternal destruction. Such men are the devil's agents. "I wrote to you," says Saint Paul, "not to keep company with fornicators. . . With such a one, not so much as to eat,"[1] and again, "put away the evil one from amongst yourselves."[2]

THE GOOD FRUITS

"Not every one that saith to me, Lord, Lord, shall enter into the kingdom of heaven: but he that doth the will of my Father who is in heaven, he shall enter into the kingdom of heaven."

---
[1] I Cor. v, 9-11. [2] Ibid., v, 13.

These words of our divine Lord, dear Brethren, teach us that it is not enough to believe in God, to belong exteriorly to the Church of Christ, to say some prayers, to perform some good works. We must observe the Commandments of God; we must fulfil with a clear conscience and with good intention for God because He so wills, the duties of our state in life. It is not enough to avoid evil, we must also do good for the love of God.

Go then and zealously do the Will of God which He makes known to you through the medium of your parents, your Superiors, the pastors of your souls, as well as by the voice of conscience.

O sweetest Jesus, grant us the necessary grace, that like good trees we may produce the fruits of virtue and thus become worthy of the Kingdom of Heaven. Amen.

Eighth Sunday after Pentecost
Luke 16, 1–9
The Great Account

> "Give an account of your stewardship."
> Luke xvi, 2.

Dear Brethren: The rich man in the Gospel is God. Heaven and earth and all things therein are His work, His property.

"The earth is the Lord's," says the Psalmist, "and the fulness thereof: the world, and all they that dwell therein."[1] Every man has been placed as steward over a small portion of this property. We have to thank God for all that we have: our souls, our bodies, life, health, riches, honor, intellect, talents: all are God's gifts, goods entrusted to us over which we have been placed as stewards, not as owners, and we shall have to render to God a strict account of our stewardship. "Give an account of your stewardship," says the rich man in the Gospel.

" GIVE AN ACCOUNT "

Brethren, give praise to God for His fatherly love. How different is He from the rulers and lords of this world. These in appointing their stewards have their own interests solely in view. But God in making us His stewards, seeks our advantage only. If you keep your accounts in good order; if you manage the household under your charge well; if you employ the years of your youth in the practice of virtue, in the fulfilment of the duties of your calling: all this is to your own advantage, your own profit. If you waste

---

[1] Ps. xxiii, 1.

God's gifts and graces and do not turn them to good account: that is your own loss.

Even as far as regards this world, what a sad future is in store for those young people, boys and girls, who instead of employing their youth in studying, in learning something by which later they may gain their own living, waste those precious days in idleness, in vain amusements. But how infinitely worse for them if this precious time of youth is spent in sin, in offending God, their greatest Benefactor.

The day of reckoning will come, we know not how soon, when each and every one of us shall stand before the Judgment Seat of God and shall be called upon to give an account of our stewardship, when each of us shall be asked: What use have you made of your body, of its members, of your health? What use have you made of your understanding, your will, your freedom? Give an account of so many divine inspirations, of so many graces given you in hearing the Word of God, in the Sacraments, of all the good which you could have done, of all the evil which you have done.

Sad indeed was the fate of the foolish Virgins who neglected to provide the oil of good works in readiness for the arrival of the Heavenly Bridegroom. And what worse fate can there be for a man than to put off the supreme business of his life, the salvation of his soul, until the hour when he shall hear those words, "Thou canst be steward no longer."

MAKE FRIENDS FOR YOURSELVES

That so when you go hence, they may receive you into the everlasting dwellings. You make friends of the poor when you assist them by your alms; you make friends of all to whom you show kindness, charity; you make friends of those to whom you make restitution by restoring ill-gotten goods; you make friends of the Saints when you serve God faithfully and imitate their virtues. They will be your advocates before God that you may persevere to the end in His divine Grace. O divine Jesus! grant us all the grace ever to make use of Thy gifts for Thy Honor, for the good of our neighbor, and the salvation of our own souls. Amen.

Ninth Sunday after Pentecost

Luke xix, 31–47

Jesus Wept

> "And when he drew near, seeing the city, he wept over it." Luke xix, 41.

DEAR BRETHREN: For the seventh time during His earthly journeyings, a few days before His Passion our divine Savior took the road to Jerusalem. On this occasion He came from Bethsaida and descending the Mount of Olives, "drew near" the city. It lay before Him, that proud city to which indeed He had so often drawn near that He might impart to it His grace, His doctrines, but which in its obduracy remained so far from its Savior, its salvation. And although the loud Hosannas of the multitudes who had come to meet Him were filling the air, yet, clearly beholding the sinful abomination of the city before Him, our divine Lord while predicting its destruction wept over its ruin.

Here we recognise in Jesus Christ two natures: the divine nature, for He foretells what no mere human being could foresee, whilst His tears reveal His human nature.

What signified these tears of Jesus? They

signified love. "See how he loved Him," exclaimed the Jews when they saw our Lord weeping at the tomb of Lazarus. But how immeasurably greater is the love here shown by our divine Savior. For it was not a friend like Lazarus over whom He mourned, but His bitterest enemies who soon would cry out "crucify him, crucify him." They were tears which were wrung from Him by anguish all the more bitter that it was not for the natural death of a dear friend that He mourned, mourning which in the case of Lazarus was by his resurrection changed into joy, but for the temporal and eternal ruin of those whom, although they were His greatest enemies, He so tenderly loved.

The anguish of parents who grieve for a child who has gone astray has somewhat of similarity to this sorrow of our divine Lord. Sorrow for the death of an innocent child can be easily borne; the thought of that child's eternal happiness and the hope of one day being re-united to him in Heaven are as balm to the wound. On the other hand, hopeless the grief caused by an undutiful child whom, in spite of all his faults, the parents still love and whose happiness and well-being they so ardently desire.

Our Lord wept for those who wept not for themselves. On one occasion whilst hearing the confession of a hardened sinner, Saint Francis wept. On being questioned as to the cause of his tears, he answered: "I weep because you do not weep." And so Jesus wept over the unhappy city because its inhabitants wept not for its wickedness. At the same time, He teaches us to weep over our own sins and those of our fellow-men, to mourn for their impending punishment. Saint Augustine says: "David sinned once and wept evermore; you are always sinning but you never weep."

These tears of Jesus are also shed in reproach; they presage the divine Vengeance. Awful are the threatenings of divine Justice, but immeasurably more awful are the tears of divine Mercy. For like the Ninivites by sincere repentance we can escape God's Justice. But Mercy abused accuses us of grace despised and proclaims inevitable malediction; similarly, the tears which rebellious children wring from their parents often presage God's malediction.

Dear Brethren, let us weep with Jesus over our own sins; let us implore of Him mercy and pardon and grace that we may sincerely and perseveringly amend our lives.

O Jesus! we implore Thee with our whole hearts not to permit that Thy sacred tears, or Thy Precious Blood should be shed in vain for us poor sinners.

Tenth Sunday after Pentecost

Luke xviii, 9–14

The Prayer of the Publican

> "And the publican, standing afar off, would not so much as lift up his eyes towards heaven; but struck his breast, saying: O God, be merciful to me a sinner." Luke xviii, 13.

Dear Brethren: Our divine Savior is the searcher of men's hearts. In the parable of to-day's Gospel, He rejects the Pharisee because of his pride whilst the publican because of his humility and sorrow for his sins is restored to grace. In this parable our Lord teaches us how we should pray that we may go "down into our house justified." Let us therefore to-day learn from this publican how we should pray that thus we may obtain grace and mercy from the Lord.

1. *The publican Stood Far Off.* The publicans or tax collectors were, as a rule, regarded by the Jews as great sinners, our Lord Himself classed them with "heathens and unbelievers."

"He who will not hear the church let him be to thee as the heathen and the publican."[1]

The poor sinner stood far off in a corner of the Temple where in his prayer and sighs of repentance he would be least disturbed. He considered himself unworthy to approach the Altar, the Holy of holies, or to stand amongst the pious worshippers. Because he humbled himself and stood afar off, God was moved to draw near him.

My Brethren: when you go into the House of God, look upon yourself because of your many sins as unworthy to appear before Him. For the powers tremble before the Majesty of God, and the Angels themselves are not pure in His sight. When at the Church-door you take holy water, excite yourself to contrition for your sins, for God only regards with favor the prayer of the humble who are humble and contrite in heart.

If you are free to choose your place in the Church, do not like the Pharisee go where all can see you, for to do this betrays pride and vanity. Do not remain near the door where it is impossible for anyone to pray devoutly, but choose a place where you can see the Altar and the priest saying Mass, and where you can

---
[1] Matt. xviii, 17.

hear and follow the preacher of the Word of God.

2. *The publican did not venture to lift up his eyes to heaven* because of his humility and his deep sense of his sinfulness. He had sinned against the angels whose interior admonitions he had not heeded, against the Saints whose pleadings for him he had rendered vain, against God Himself whose Commandments he had violated of his own free will. But because he did not dare to raise his eyes to heaven, he drew down upon himself the gracious regards of the Lord.

Many people complain of distractions in prayer, but in most cases they are themselves to blame. They hurry to the church without the least attempt at recollection, and then, one has only to look at their eyes turning in all directions; every time the church door opens, at the least noise or movement they look round, they want to see everything, who comes in, who goes out, how this or that one is dressed. Oh! when you pray, mind yourself only and do all in your power to keep your thoughts fixed on God.

The publican Struck His Breast. By this act he acknowledged that he deserved blows and stripes from God. He struck his breast because he laid the blame for his sins on himself alone, and did not want to impute blame to others. Dear Brethren: let us also, at Mass and at Benediction, strike our breasts and thus acknowledge that we are poor sinners but that we are heartily sorry for our sins.

The publican said: "God be merciful to me a sinner." Lay it well to heart how the publican acted to obtain pardon of his sins. He acknowledged the enormity of his sins; he repented of all his offences from love of God; he even made public confession of these, for he struck his breast and said: "God be merciful to me a sinner." What a beautiful example for all penitents! Go you and do likewise.

Finally, listen now to the divine Judge who pronounces sentence on these two men. "I say to you this man (the repentant publican) went down into his house justified rather than the other: (the proud Pharisee) because everyone that exalts himself shall be humbled: and he that humbles himself shall be exalted."

Beware of pride; love humility. Amen.

Eleventh Sunday after Pentecost

Mark vii, 31–37

Cure of the Man Who Was Deaf and Dumb

> "And they bring to him one deaf and dumb."
> Mark vii, 32.

DEAR BRETHREN: What must have been the joy of this man of whom we read in to-day's Gospel, when by the Almightly Power and goodness of Jesus he was suddenly cured; when he found himself able to hear and to speak. What care he must have taken not to abuse this gift of hearing and of speech. What good use he must have made of these two gifts for God's honor and his own salvation.

But there are many who in a spiritual sense are deaf and dumb, and who most urgently need to be brought to Jesus that they might be cured. The man who will not hear the word of God, the call to penance, is deaf. When our Lord so often said, "he who has ears to hear, let him hear" or "they have ears and hear not," He had in view those who were in a spiritual sense deaf. And in this world how many are deaf. They avoid hearing the word of God, or they hear it quite unmoved; they keep away from those who would give them wholesome admonitions; they even hate to hear them; they pay no attention to the priest's exhortations in Confession.

Complete deafness is an image of the utterly hardened sinner. Just as the deaf man who is completely deaf does not perceive the most violent noise, the loudest cries, so the hardened sinner finally becomes apathetic; you may speak to him of Heaven and of hell; his conscience may be stained with sins of the deepest dye; God may inflict the severest chastisements; nothing has any effect upon him. On the other hand, he can listen attentively to flatterers, to blasphemers, calumniators, to every kind of scandalous talk.

The man who will not acknowledge his sins in Confession; who will not speak to God in prayer, or who speaks with his lips only and not with his heart: that man is dumb. He who will not defend the things of God and the Church, Faith and Virtue, he is dumb; he who like a dumb dog which cannot bark, neglects to instruct and exhort as in duty bound his children and dependents; he is dumb. And yet how eloquent such people often are when Satan rules their tongues, to boast, to calumniate, to corrupt.

Oh! how difficult it is, my Brethren, to soften

such perverse sinners in order to lead them to amend their lives. How is it to be done?

We must bring them to Jesus who alone can help. Just as the deaf and dumb man did not himself understand the utter misery of his state nor where he could find help, so those who are spiritually deaf and dumb do not perceive their misery, the devil blinds them to their state.

But we must not remit our efforts to bring these deluded men to the right road; if our efforts fail, we must do like the friends of the man who was deaf and dumb. Because he could not pray, they prayed for him. Let us often and fervently plead with our divine Lord for the conversion of sinners, but before all for our own conversion. "Open thy mouth for the dumb, . . . do Justice to the needy and the poor."[1]

In conclusion, the Evangelist relates how the people filled with wonder praised the Lord. " He hath done all things well; he hath made both the deaf to hear and the dumb to speak."

Dear Brethren: Let us also praise God in all His work. For, " we know that to them that love God, all things work together unto good, . . . [2] And as we shall one day be asked whether we

---

[1] Prov. xxxi, 8-9.   [2] Rom. viii, 28.

have in our life done all things well, let us, therefore, take care that we do all that God wills, because He wills it, and as He wills. Let God be in our hearts by His grace, in our thoughts according to His Will, before our eyes in His presence. "Walk before me and be perfect."[1]

Twelfth Sunday after Pentecost

Luke x, 23-27

The Most Important Question of Life

> "Master, what must I do to possess eternal life?"
> Luke x, 25.

Dear Brethren: In to-day's Gospel, our Lord says of His disciples, "Blessed are the eyes that see the things which you see." Like the disciples whom our Lord thus praises, we too may be called blessed.

We should constantly thank God that we are children of the Catholic Church, and that we participate in all those graces and in the Sacraments which secure our eternal salvation. But at the same time we have also to find the really right solution of the most important question of life which confronts us in to-day's Gospel.

---
[1] Gen. i, 17.

1. *Question.* " What must I do to possess eternal life?"

My Brethren: time and with it all earthly things are rapidly passing away, never halting for one moment. Soon and unexpectedly we shall reach the confines of life in this world. If we would not that death should find us unprepared for his coming, we must often ask ourselves this most important question: What must I do to gain eternal life? Many men neglect to do good and commit all kinds of sin, because they so seldom think of their own death and of eternal life.

Therefore, every morning, ask yourselves: If I were to die to-day unexpectedly what have I to expect in Eternity? Reward or punishment? At night, before you go to sleep, ask yourselves " What would be my fate, if my awakening were in Eternity?"

II. *Answer to This All-important Question:* " Thou shalt love the Lord thy God with thy whole heart, and with thy whole soul, and with all thy strength, and with all thy mind, and thy neighbor as thyself."

You must love God; that means that you must find delight, joy, pleasure in God Who is the Supreme Good. Justly does He deserve our love, for He is an all-powerful, all-knowing, ever-present, merciful, but at the same time, just Father. He is the source of all good, all beauty, of all that is worthy of love. We have to thank Him for our souls, our bodies, and all that we possess. "For in Him we live, and move, and are."

Whom then shall we love, if we refuse our love to the Supreme Good? Therefore, Brethren, love God.

1. *With Thy Whole Heart.* It must not be a divided heart. If you to-day rejoice in God, avoid deliberate sin, and try to please Him, but to-morrow, in a moment of temptation or in suffering or sorrow, you forget your Creator, sin deliberately, and prefer miserable creatures to Him: then you love God with a divided heart.

2. *With thy whole soul:* that is to say all the powers of your soul must be employed in serving and honoring God. You employ your understanding in honoring Him when you constantly strive to advance in the knowledge of God and of the truths which He has revealed. Therefore, be diligent in attending sermons in order to hear the word of God. You employ your will in honoring God when you desire nothing so much

as to serve Him, and detest nothing so much as sin and vice. You employ your memory in honoring Him when you often willingly think of God and of divine things.

With Thy Whole Strength. We should love God not only in words, but we must also serve Him by our actions, and not deny Him by our works.

With All Thy Mind. All the emotions of our nature, love, joy, sorrow, contrition, desire should only serve for the honor and glory of God. God alone must be the object of all our wishes, all our desires, the center of our souls.

Now, dear Brethren, often ask yourselves: Do I indeed frequently think of the presence of God, of my beloved heavenly Father? Do I perform all my work for His honor and for love of Him? Am I firmly resolved to suffer everything rather than offend God by one deliberate sin?

O most loving God and Father! inflame our hearts with the most ardent love of Thee that we may always serve Thee faithfully and be united with Thee for all eternity. Amen.

Thirteenth Sunday after Pentecost
Luke xvii, 11–19

Before and After Confession

> "Jesus, master, have mercy on us." Luke xvii, 13.

DEAR BRETHREN: The ten lepers in to-day's Gospel teach us that to be saved from the deadly leprosy of sin, we should with great earnestness have recourse to Him Who is the best physician for all maladies of soul and body, at the same time crying out: "Jesus, master, have mercy on us!" To this end the Lord has given us the Sacrament of Penance by which we may be perfectly healed of the leprosy of sin. What shall we do to attain this end?

I. BEFORE CONFESSION

The frightful disease of leprosy is an image of sin, especially the sin of impurity by which men render themselves an abomination in the sight of God.[1] Leprosy by degrees affects the entire body; similarly the sin of impurity affects the whole soul. It blinds the understanding so that it no longer heeds the Presence of God or the admonitions of Religion. The impure shall not enter Heaven; even in this world God often

---
[1] Ps. xiii, 1.

punishes the impure with frightful diseases and untimely deaths.

If you would not be contaminated by the leprosy of sin, fly dissolute, depraved company, otherwise you cannot save your soul but will perish in the danger. Sad experiences confirm this truth.

2. But when one has fallen, where is help to be found? The ten lepers have found out, and they point to Jesus Christ "Jesus, master, have mercy on us." Thus we pray before going to Confession and our divine Redeemer says to us, "Go, show yourselves to the priests."

The sins of all those who are truly penitent are remitted when the priest pronounces absolution. For this divine power was given by our Savior to the Apostles and their successors, the priests of His Church, when he said, "Whose sins you shall forgive, they are forgiven, and whose sins you shall retain, they are retained." [1]

Dear Brethren, if you have made one false step or many, about which you are troubled, go as soon as possible to confession and make known your faults truthfully and with sincere repentance to a priest whom you are free to choose. Do not

[1] John xx, 23.

put off this important step from one time to another, for God has never promised you to-morrow. The ten lepers quickly obeyed our divine Savior and went to the priests, and they were rewarded for their obedience. Do you likewise, and thus secure your salvation; then you can say with David. "I have acknowledged my sin to Thee, and my injustice I have not concealed."

II. AFTER CONFESSION

"Were not ten made clean? and where are the nine?" Such was the reproach uttered by our divine Lord when only one of the lepers whom He had healed returned to thank Him.

How beautiful and touching is the . . . gratitude of this Samaritan. How frightful the ingratitude of those nine others who were Jews! How sad it is that so frequently amongst ten men we find one alone truly grateful.

Ah! how many children forget the benefits they have received from their parents. How many rail at their spiritual guides. What pain is caused by ingratitude. But alas! ingratitude is the return of this world for benefits.

Dear Brethren, beware, especially, of ingratitude to our Lord after confession. He has given you the great grace of true contrition and sincere confession. God has remitted to you all your sins, no matter how great or how many; you have been released from the eternal punishment due to your sins, and according to the measure of your repentance, you have been released also from the temporal punishment. Peace of conscience which through sin you had lost, is now restored to you.

From being children of wrath, you have become friends of God, what greater benefit could you receive? How great, therefore, should be your gratitude.

After Confession, do not leave the church immediately, but having received Absolution, like the grateful Samaritan, fall down at our Lord's feet, return thanks to your divine Savior for having cleansed you from the leprosy of sin and restored you to His grace. Ah! how many Christians are there who notwithstanding their confessions have gone to destruction. Ingratitude has been the cause of their relapse into their former sins.

O dearest Jesus! grant us the grace to thank you our whole lives long for the remission of our sins, and also grant that we may praise and thank you for ever in Heaven. Amen.

Fourteenth Sunday after Pentecost

Matt. vi, 33

Worldliness—Worldly Cares

> "Seek ye therefore first the kingdom of God, and his justice, and all these things shall be added unto you."
> Matt. vi, 33.

Dear Brethren: To-day our divine Savior would free us from a sad slavery which binds men with heavy chains, that slavery is: worldliness and worldly cares, the service of the world and the cares of the world. Many think they can serve both God and this sinful world. But our Lord says: "No man can serve two masters." These words are as a thunderbolt for so many who think that they can serve two masters. Others are so exceedingly anxious, so full of care about the things of this world, temporal goods, that they make these temporal things the chief aim of life. And the result is utter failure.

Let us learn from our Lord how we may find the right medium.

SERVING THE WORLD

"No man can serve two masters. For either he will hate the one, and love the other: or he will sustain the one, and despise the other. You cannot serve God and mammon."

Therefore, dear Brethren, we cannot follow both the commandments of God and the corrupt principles of the world, because what God wills us to do is nearly always in direct opposition to what the world would have us do; the world generally wants from us what God forbids. If you would serve Almighty God, you must renounce the service of the world, the flesh, and the devil.

The foolish worldling says: your first thought when you awake should be of money, how you are to grow rich; it will be time enough to serve God in your old age. But Jesus Christ commands us to love God above all things and to give Him the first fruits of the day and of our youth.

The world says: Unless a man is rich he cannot be happy or content. Covetous worldlings are always striving even on Sundays and holy days for temporal gain, and they neglect to go to Mass, or if they do go, their hearts even in the House of God are wholly taken up with their business affairs. But God has said: "Seek ye first the kingdom of God and all these things shall be added to you"—that is to say, His blessing will be upon your labors.

The Philistines once put the Ark of the Covenant, so sacred to the Israelites, in the temple beside their false god Dagon, but God was jealous for His Honor; on the next day, in the early morning, they found their idol lying broken into pieces on the ground before the Ark of God. From this, dear Brethren, we learn in what detestation God holds those who place their evil passions beside their God on the altar of their hearts, and who would unite on the same spot Christ and Belial, the service of God and that of the world, sensuality and purity, virtue and vice.

God will never take up His abode in such a heart which as a temple of false gods will be an abomination in His sight. Christ can have no fellowship with Belial.

WORLDLY CARES AND ANXIETIES

Our divine Savior does not forbid us to provide for food and raiment, but He condemns that excessive anxiety about these things which lessens, or wholly does away with our trust in God's fatherly Providence. Jesus Christ Himself, until His thirtieth year, worked at the carpenter's bench with His foster-father, and St. Paul says: "if any man will not work, neither let him eat."[1]

We must find the right medium; we must work as diligently as if everything depended on our own efforts, and at the same time place all our trust in God, as if all our success depended on His loving Providence and all-powerful help.

How beautiful are the words of David:[2] "In Thee have our fathers hoped, they have hoped, and thou hast delivered them, they cried to thee and were saved: they trusted in thee and were not confounded."

How touching the comparisons drawn by our divine Lord: "Behold the birds of the air, for they neither sow, nor do they reap, nor gather into barns: and your heavenly Father feedeth them. Are not you of much more value than they?"

"And for raiment why are you solicitous? Consider the lilies of the field how they grow: they labor not, neither do they spin. But I say to you, that not even Solomon in all his glory was arrayed as one of these."

Jesus exhorts His disciples to contemplate

---

[1] II Thess. iii, 10.   [2] Ps. xxi, 5–6.

Nature and thus teaches us all to cast off excessive care for temporal things and to strive first of all for the everlasting riches of Heaven, to seek after the Justice of God, to avoid evil, and to do good.

O most loving Jesus! our most fervent prayer is that our chief care may ever be to increase in virtue, to walk according to Thy teaching and example and to prepare ourselves for an eternity of happiness. Amen.

Fifteenth Sunday after Pentecost

Luke vii, 11–16

The Angel of Death and the Lord of Life

> "Behold, a dead man was carried out . . ."
> Luke vii, 12.

Dear Brethren: In a moment, on this very day, at a sign from God, the Angel of death in obedience to Him would carry our souls to His Judgment seat. But listen to the Lord of Life. Moved by the sorrow of the desolate widow mourning for her only son as she walked behind his bier, Jesus said to the dead youth " Young man, I say to thee, arise." And immediately, the dead youth arose from his bier and began to speak. What precious lesson is this miracle intended to convey to us?

I. "A DEAD MAN WAS CARRIED OUT"

This boy had been cut off in the very flower of his youth when nothing was so far from his thoughts as death, eternity.

O young men, young girls, you are building too much on your health, your youth; you think of death as of something very far from you, and yet, death may be, perhaps, very near you; your life hangs, as it were, upon a thread which at any moment, may break. More die under thirty years of age than over.

Keep your young souls free from sin, and then, you will find it easy to die, even in your youth. But if death for each and every one of us is certain, so is the hour in which we must die uncertain. We know not the year, the day, nor the hour, nor do we know whether we shall die in the grace of God or in mortal sin.

And yet, so few think seriously of death.

Why does God keep the hour of our going hence such a secret? That we may be always ready, says St. Augustine, to leave this world. "Watch, therefore," says Jesus Christ, "for in an hour that ye think not the Son of man cometh."[1]

O Lord, deliver us from a sudden and unprovided death.

II. "WEEP NOT"

By these tender words the Son of God would console the grief-stricken widowed mother, and at the same time teach us that we should not grieve immoderately at the death of a good Christian. The Apostle, likewise, admonishes us that we should not mourn like the heathens who have no hope because they do not believe in the resurrection of the dead.

We may indeed weep, for he who would forbid weeping must first do away with affliction. As blood flows from bodily wounds, so does the flood of tears pour from the wounded heart. But whilst we weep, as good Christians we must hope in the help of the Lord.

Oh! Brethren, behold the compassionate Heart of Jesus, "being moved with mercy towards her," says the Gospel. If you are overwhelmed by great distress and trouble, and all hearts are closed against you, see, there is one heart which

---
[1] Luke xii, 40–45; Matt. xxiv, 44.

compassionates you, the Heart of God made Man, of Jesus Christ. "For we have not a high priest, who can not have compassion on our infirmities: but one tempted in all things like as we are, without sin. Let us go therefore with confidence to the throne of grace: that we may obtain mercy, and find grace in seasonable aid."[1]

Jesus, the All-Merciful God, is now and always the true consoler of those who mourn. The widow of Naim experienced this. How foolishly those act who seek for consolation elsewhere than in Jesus Christ.

III. "YOUNG MAN, I SAY TO THEE ARISE"

And the dead man sat up and began to speak. My Brethren: God alone can speak thus, for God alone "quickeneth the dead; and calleth those things that are not, as those that are."[2]

By this great, public miracle Jesus once more manifests His divine Power, and we must prostrate ourselves before Him; we must adore Him and render Him divine honor.

"I say to thee, arise." This is the exhortation which Jesus Christ who has come to seek and to save that which was lost, for ever addresses

---
[1] Heb. iv, 15–16.   [2] Rom. iv, 17.

to sinners. Alas! how many are there to whom the reproach which God makes by the mouth of His Prophet, applies " I called, and there was none that would answer; I have spoken, and they heard not; and they have done evil in my eyes, and have chosen the things that displease me." [1]

But wo to those unhappy souls who heed not the call to grace of Jesus who offers them life and salvation. Not every day does Jesus come "to the gate of the city," and when He comes for the unbeliever, then does He come in Judgment.

O Lord Jesus! justly are we ashamed, for the dead hear Thy word and obey it, whilst we are insensible to Thy inspirations, deaf to the teachings of Thy Gospel, and disobedient to our pastors and parents. Oh! awaken us from the deathlike sleep of tepidity, and help us that we may be ever well-prepared to appear before thy Judgment seat. Amen.

[1] Ps. lxvi, 4.

Sixteenth Sunday after Pentecost

Luke xiv, 1–11

Sanctification of the Sunday

> "Is it lawful to heal on the Sabbath?" Luke xiv, 3.

DEAR BRETHREN: In to-day's Gospel we find our divine Savior invited to dinner by a rich Pharisee. St. Luke remarks that they watched him closely to try to discover something in His speech or in His actions with which to reproach Him and to lessen Him in the esteem of the people. So evil were their hearts.

We wish also to watch our dear Lord in order to learn the beautiful lessons He gives us, that so we may follow Him and work out our eternal salvation. Let us take but one lesson from the question: Is it lawful to heal on the Sabbath? This question concerns the sanctification of the Sunday.

I. THE LORD'S DAY

In the old Covenant, God had so strictly commanded the Jews to keep the Sabbath holy that they were forbidden under penalty of death to perform any servile work on that day. God

PENTECOST

ordered a man to be stoned to death because on the Sabbath he had gathered a little wood.[1]

In the New Covenant instead of the Sabbath, Sunday has become the Lord's Day, and the Church teaches what we should do on that day and what we should leave undone.

What then is Sunday? Sunday is the commemoration day of God's work in the Creation; therefore it is the Christian's duty on this day to admire and to adore God's Almighty Power, His Wisdom, His love, and to thank Him for having created us rational beings and in His own image and likeness. It is the Commemoration Day of our Redemption on which we thank the Son of God for His life and death by which He offered Himself for us that we being freed from sin and delivered from Hell might be everlastingly happy. We commemorate this great work of charity in the Mass at which we are bound to assist devoutly on Sundays.

It is the *Commemoration Day* of our Lord's Resurrection which is the pledge of our own

---

[1] "And it came to pass, when the children of Israel were in the wilderness, and had found a man gathering sticks on the sabbath day. And the Lord said to Moses: Let that man die, let all the multitude stone him without the camp." Numb. 15, 32-36.

resurrection, therefore we must on this day raise our thoughts to Heaven where we shall attain our everlasting destiny. It is a day of rest for our bodies, a day of rest from earthly affairs, a day to be devoted to our souls and the affairs of our eternal salvation with which on this day we should be particularly occupied.

Because of the solemn significance of Sunday, the Church obliges us to keep this day of the Lord holy, and strictly commands us to hear Mass with due devotion and to refrain from servile work.

The entire day belongs to the Lord; we should, therefore, diligently attend the Word of God by hearing sermons and instructions; we should approach the Sacraments and perform works of charity, and so glorify God and sanctify our souls. Do we all keep Sunday in this manner?

II. THE ABUSE OF SUNDAY

Alas! for many Christians the Lord's Day is:

1. *A day of labor* the same as any other day of the week, a day devoted to the same thoughts, the same temporal cares and business, not from necessity, but solely from covetousness, a day

of servile work. Can we wonder if God reciprocates this action and that men, notwithstanding all their efforts, for want of His blessing fall deeper and deeper into want and misery.

2. A day given up to Satan to whom on Sundays and festivals more sacrifice is offered, more souls seduced than on any other day of the week; on that day the drunkard indulges in his orgies, the libertine wallows in vice and even desecrates the sanctuary with his foul presence; on that day the gambling table collects its slaves; on that day, the abandoned crew of unbelievers gather together to mock at God and the Church, to interchange their hellish principles, to seduce the novice; on that day pride holds its triumphal procession and in its wake follow envy and calumny; on that day the devil often sows the seeds of revenge and deadly enmity in men's hearts.

Ah! May God have mercy on us. For many Christians Sunday is no longer the Lord's Day, but the devil's market-day and the carnival of Hell, because they do not serve God, but expedite rather the eternal ruin of their souls.

Dear Brethren, on Sundays, forget the sinful strivings of the world and devote the Lord's

Day wholly to Religion. Zealously hear the Word of God, and remember that you have been created solely to serve God and to love Him. Examine your conscience with regard to the week that has passed; receive the Sacraments devoutly; hold fast to your holy Faith, and continue in the faithful love of Jesus until your happy end. Amen.

Seventeenth Sunday after Pentecost

Matt. xxii, 35-36

The Two Great Questions

> "Master, which is the great commandment in the law? What think you of Christ?"
> Matt. xxii, 33, 42.

Dear Brethren: To-day's Gospel contains for us a two-fold lesson which is of far greater value than all the knowledge and wisdom of the world, for it tells us in a few words what we must believe and what we must do to please God, and thus attain eternal life. There are two questions:

1. *"Master which is the great Commandment in the Law?"*

The Pharisees only wanted to entrap our Lord. In their laws they had 600 commandments, therefore one of the most learned amongst them put this question to Him.

Our divine Savior knew their evil design, and yet, for our instruction He answered in a friendly manner.

"*Thou shalt love the Lord thy God with thy whole heart, and with thy whole soul, and with thy whole mind.* This is the greatest and the first commandment. And the second is like to this: *Thou shalt love thy neighbor as thyself.* On these two commandments dependeth the whole law and the prophets."

Thus, dear Brethren, you see that charity is the essence of all the commandments imposed on us. Neither Moses nor the Prophets, nor Jesus nor the Apostles are satisfied with mere pious desires; all insist that our love of God and our neighbor must be practical, fruitful in works.

Therefore, to-morrow morning on your awakening, reanimate your love of God by fervent prayer; often during the day and especially at night before you sleep give expression to this love.

"My God, grant me the grace to love Thee; strengthen my weakness that I may never wilfully transgress Thy Commandments." You must also love every man as yourself; you must show this love not only in words but much more in deeds. Begrudge no man therefore, the privileges which you yourself enjoy. When he is in trouble, act towards him as you wish others to act towards you if you were in the same position. To accept services from others, and to be unwilling to help them is despicable. To be willing to receive and unwilling to give is not charitable.

As we all very often sin against the love of God and of our neighbor, everyone of us has reason to cry out every day: O my God! pardon my countless sins against charity. I am now firmly resolved, O my God! to love Thee above all things and my neighbor as myself. Assist me with thy all-powerful grace to be faithful to my resolution.

II. "WHAT THINK YOU OF CHRIST?"

As the time drew near when Jesus should suffer and die, He wished to teach the Jews that the Messiah was not merely the human son and descendant of the great King David, but was at one and the same time true God and true Man.

This knowledge, this belief in the Divinity of Jesus Christ is necessary for all those who would attain to eternal life. Therefore our Lord says to all the Faithful. "I am the way, the truth, and the life. No man cometh to the Father but by me." [1]

2. We, my dear brethren, have the supreme happiness of possessing the true faith, and we acknowledge and recognize Jesus Christ as the Son of the living God. But what will this grace profit us if we do not obey His teaching, if we divide our hearts between God and the world; if we, at one time cling to the highest good, at another to the lowest vices? What help will it be to us one day before the Judgment Seat of God, if we at one time helped our neighbor, and at another treated him unkindly and with contempt?

O Jesus, strengthen us, weak creatures as we are, with Thy grace that we may love Thee above all things and our neighbor as ourselves, and that we may continue thus to love Thee throughout Eternity in Heaven. Amen.

---

[1] John xiv, 6.

Eighteenth Sunday after Pentecost

Matt. ix, 1–8

Healing of the Man Sick with Palsy

> "And behold they brought to him one sick of the palsy."
> Matt. ix, 2.

DEAR BRETHREN: In to-day's Gospel as we read the miracle wrought by our Lord upon the man suffering from palsy, we recognize in Him three divine attributes: divine Mercy, Omniscience and Power. As we consider these, may the Holy Ghost fill our hearts with the most fervent love of Jesus, and strengthen our confidence in prayer.

I. THE DIVINE MERCY

The palsied man by his sins had brought this grievous malady upon himself. Our Lord, touched by the charity of those who had brought the sick man lying on his bed, and by his sincere repentance, said to him: "Be of good heart, son, thy sins are forgiven thee." Two-fold mercy! He pardons all his sins, remits the punishment due to them, and accepts him as His son.

Our Lord and Savior here shows Himself as our Redeemer Who has power to forgive sin. To-day, He speaks the same words to all sinners who with sincere sorrow confess their sins to a priest. "Be comforted, son, daughter, thy sins are forgiven thee." For he has said to the priests. "Whose sins you shall forgive, they are forgiven." [1]

We thank Thee, dearest Lord, that Thou hast given us the Sacrament of Penance whereby the wounds which sin has caused in our souls may be healed.

II. JESUS, DIVINE OMNISCIENCE

At the words, "thy sins are forgiven thee," the Scribes were angry, and said to one another, "He blasphemeth. God alone can forgive sin. He makes himself God." But although in their hearts they thought this, they did not say it aloud.

Our divine savior, omniscient as He is, knew their thoughts and He said to them. "Why do you think evil in your hearts?" He is the searcher of hearts; He knows the hearts of all men.

---
[1] John xx, 23.

Dear Brethren: when you wilfully entertain vain, proud, envious, avaricious, impure, angry, and revengeful thoughts, God by the voice of your conscience says to you: Why do you think evil in your hearts? God knows your hearts far better than you know them yourselves. Encourage therefore, good dispositions; cherish good desires in your hearts; our Lord takes note of them all in order to reward them in the future. Do not allow evil thoughts and vicious desires to creep into your heart nor to find therein the least resting-place, for our Lord will note them for your future punishment. On the Judgment Day He "will bring to light the hidden things of darkness, and will make manifest the counsels of the hearts; and then shall every man have praise from God." [1]

Then shall each one receive what is due to Him.

III. JESUS, DIVINE OMNIPOTENCE

Our Lord in the cure of the man suffering from palsy manifested His divine Omnipotence when He said to him. "Arise, take up thy bed, and go into thy house."

---

[1] I Cor. iv, 5.

This miracle wrought before a multitude of people was a certain proof that the sick man's sins had been remitted, and that Jesus was the Almighty Lord of sickness and health, of life and of death. And in order that no one could doubt of the sick man's perfect cure, He commanded him to arise, and even to take his bed on his shoulders and to go to his house, which he did at once.

My Brethren, lay to heart the beautiful words of St. Bernard. "Doubt not, O Christian, that you have been purified from your sins at Confession, if you arise from the sleep of sin, if you carry away from evil desires the bed of your body; for then, you are sure to go into the house of eternal bliss."

Nineteenth Sunday after Pentecost

Matt. xxii, 1–14

The Happiness of Catholics

> "Tell them that were invited: come ye to the marriage."
> Matt. xxii, 4.

Dear Brethren: The meaning of the beautiful parable in to-day's Gospel is: The King is God the Father, the King's Son is Jesus

Christ, the banquet hall is the Catholic Church, the marriage feast is the voluntary acceptance and faithful following of the Catholic Religion, and the eternal happiness which it entails. The guests invited first were the Jews, but they would not accept the invitation and murdered the King's son.

We Catholics are the fortunate guests, for we have been invited to the Marriage Feast of the Lamb and participate therein. Let us consider, to-day, our priceless happiness.

1. At this Marriage Feast the most Holy Body of Jesus Christ the Lamb of God is our food, and His Precious Blood our drink. He invites us all to His mystical Banquet, and even threatens us that if we do not appear at it we shall be deprived of eternal Life.

" Amen, amen, I say unto you, except you eat the flesh of the son of man, and drink his blood, you shall not have life in you. I am the living bread, which came down from heaven. If any man eat of this bread, he shall live for ever; "

What little impression these words make upon so many Christians. They seldom appear at the divine Banquet to which in the Adorable Sacrament of the Altar Jesus invites them.

Sometimes they say: I have no time, or I am not worthy to receive Holy Communion, or they make some other excuse. But such excuses avail as little with the divine Host and Eternal Judge as did the excuses of the thankless guests in to-day's Gospel.

You know, dear Brethren, that our late Holy Father, Pius X, urged upon all the Faithful the very frequent reception of Holy Communion; indeed, he urged them, when circumstances permitted, to communicate daily. It is seldom that those, who from pure negligence or want of appreciation put off for a long time the receiving of this divine Food, are able to remain in the state of grace.

Some good Catholics have been heard to say: "I must go to the Sacraments, I feel so little strength against temptation that I am afraid of falling. But when I receive Holy Communion I feel strong enough to overcome all the enemies of my soul." St. Paul says the same: "I can do all things in him who strengtheneth me." [1]

But our divine Savior requires that each of His guests should have a wedding garment,

---
[1] Phil. 4, 13.

that is to say, they must be in the state of grace. At your Baptism, you all received this robe of sanctifying grace whereby Heaven was opened to you as the children of God. Blessed are those who have kept this garment unstained, Oh! watch, take care that for no sinful pleasure, no earthly advantage will you stain with grievous sin this beautiful robe of baptismal innocence.

If anyone should appear before God, the King of kings, in a garment stained with mortal sin, his punishment is foretold in to-day's Gospel, unless he does penance for his transgressions. " Bind his hands and feet, and cast him into the exterior darkness: there shall be weeping and gnashing of teeth." That is into Hell, which is the place of eternal punishment for those who die in mortal sin.

We have all of us as Catholics the sweetest happiness of being called to the eternal Marriage Feast of the Lamb. Give thanks to the Lord who has vouchsafed to grant us through no merit of ours this grace. But preserve this gift as the Apostle St. Peter [1] exhorts us to do. " Wherefore, brethren, labor the more, that by

---

[1] II, i, 10.

good works you may make sure your calling and election." Pray often and fervently for the grace of perseverance, and then with confidence trust in the Lord and His mercy. Amen.

Twentieth Sunday after Pentecost
John iv, 45-53

> "and himself believed, and his whole house."
> John iv, 53.

Dear Brethren: The wonderful miracle of which we read in to-day's Gospel reveals to us the Almighty power of Jesus Christ Who can heal the sick, even when far away from Him. The royal official with his high-sounding title and his riches was powerless to help his son who lay sick unto death. And because the physicians could do nothing, and no man could advise him, he turned at last, although a heathen, to our divine Savior. And thus, you see his son's illness instead of being a misfortune proved a most fortunate occurrence, for it afforded him an opportunity of knowing Jesus Christ better, of accepting His teaching, and it brought happiness to himself and his family.

May we, dear Brethren, ever preserve this

happiness of the living faith, let us pray to-day for this great grace, and let us from this ruler in the Gospel learn a lesson.

I. HE BELIEVES

How did this high official come to seek Jesus?

1. He had never seen our Lord work a miracle, nor had he heard any stories which might inspire him with confidence. He availed himself of the opportunity; he knew our Lord was in the neighborhood; he hoped for help from Him, therefore he lost no time but went at once to Him.

We, my Brethren, also know well that we are always near our Lord, but we do not give ourselves much trouble to avail ourselves of the opportunity afforded for the healing of our souls from their sins. And yet, who knows if this time of grace, of inspirations will ever come for us again? The early Christians dug caves in the ground in which they assembled at the risk of their lives to celebrate the divine Mysteries; many Catholics go a day's journey to reach a church, whilst so many worldlings scarcely enter the church although near to them, on the greatest Festivals, and even at Easter, make no effort to examine their consciences. Will they not have a strict account to render to God?

2. *Misfortune Led Him to Jesus.* Let us recognize in this the great importance of suffering as a means used by our loving God for our spiritual progress. "Such as I love, I rebuke and chastise. Be zealous therefore, and do penance." [1]

Hence, not to be willing to amend our lives, even at the cost of suffering, would be a sign of great hardness of heart.

3. He went himself to our Lord and besought His help. It is indeed fitting that the parents themselves should look after the welfare of the souls of their children, when they leave nothing undone for the health of their bodies.

4. *He Went Quickly.* Let us hasten also, for we are all advancing rapidly to death; let us implore our Lord to come to us with His grace that death may not overtake us far away from Him.

Our Lord rewarded the humble supplicant, and said to him: "Go thy way; thy son liveth." And at once he went away, and he found in truth

---

[1] Apoc. iii, 19.

his son who was sick unto death, restored to perfect health, and he believed.

II. WITH HIS WHOLE HOUSE

This therefore was a two-fold miracle: the sick youth made well suddenly, and the father with his whole family converted to belief in the Son of God.

The father now become a believer would not have a son who believed differently, nor an unbelieving servant in his house. Christian parents, learn from this that your God-given vocation is to be the guides of all those belonging to you in the way of all good. Many commit sin by neglecting to give edifying example and good lessons to their children, or even by leading them astray, by instilling principles of unbelief and teaching them profligacy. Wo to such parents! Better that a mill-stone were tied round their necks and that they were cast into the depths of the sea than give such scandal.

Dear Brethren, where is there a house, a family, which does not owe a thousand-fold gratitude to God for benefits received?

Therefore let us gladly discharge our great debt of thanksgiving by our faith and loyal service; each one with his family. Amen.

Twenty-first Sunday after Pentecost

Matt. xviii, 25–35

How Ready God is to Forgive

> "And the lord of that servant being moved with pity, let him go and forgave him the debt." Matt. xviii, 27.

DEAR BRETHREN: At the end of our lives, we shall all of us have to render an account as servants to the King of Kings, our Lord Jesus Christ, of the goods which have been entrusted to us, how we have used them both as regards God's honor and our own salvation. St. Augustine says: "If in the sight of God no mortal man will be found guiltless, however just and pious he may have always been, then every one has cause to fear the divine Judgment."

But in to-day's Gospel, we see how ready God is to pardon us all, if we ask Him, and if we freely forgive our neighbor.

WE ARE GREAT DEBTORS

1. The servant in the Gospel owed his master ten thousand talents, about 10,000,000 dollars.

Our debts to God are not small, rather are they of very great amount. If a man only committed one fault each day, in twenty years his sins would amount to 7300. Alas! people sin many times during the day, at one time by thoughts and desires, at another by doing wrong and omitting to do good, sometimes by their own sins, and sometimes through the sin of others. Who is there who cannot with David cry out "my iniquities have overtaken me, they are multiplied above the hairs of my head."

How great beyond all calculation is one, only one, deliberate grievous sin, for man in the sight of God is a poor, wretched creature, a worm of the earth, dust quickened into life. And he sins in the Presence of God before Whose Majesty the Seraphim tremble. If God treated us as we deserve for our sins, we should all perish.

But no matter how great may be the debt of sin which we owe to God, we need never despair or be discouraged, for God's mercy is greater than our sinfulness. Our divine Savior reveals this to us in the beautiful parable in which the servant only asked for a short time in which to pay what he owed, and the master granted him far more than he asked by cancelling the debt in full.

By this parable, our Lord encourages all, even the greatest sinners, to turn to God Who in the excess of His tender love is ever ready to forgive all penitents their debt of sin. "Remember Rachab," says Saint Chrysostom, "who was an unfaithful wife, and yet she was saved from destruction. The thief on the Cross was a murderer as well as a thief, and yet he became an inhabitant of Heaven. The publican became one of the Evangelists, and a persecutor of the Church was changed into an Apostle. What powerful reasons for confidence in God!"

But, dear Brethren, God also sets before us clearly

II. THE CONDITIONS OF FORGIVENESS

1. Humbly implore God's forgiveness. With the debtor in the Gospel cry our: "Lord have patience with me, and I will pay thee all." With sincere sorrow bewail that you have so often and so grievously offended God, your greatest Benefactor; that you have preferred creatures to Him, that you have abandoned the fountain of living waters, and have dug a cistern for yourself which holds no water [1] but only

---
[1] Jerem. 7, 13.

loathsome mud. Then make known your sins to the priest, and do all in your power to amend your life and to strengthen yourself in virtue.

2. *Also, Forgive Your Neighbor.* We are indeed filled with indignation against the servant whose own enormous debt was cancelled by his master, and yet who will not himself forgive his fellow-servant. We admit that he deserved eternal punishment. But alas! even amongst us Christians we find similar sad examples. God listens to the petition of a mortal, but how many Christians are deaf to the pleadings of their fellow-men who are in want. God remits to us when we humble ourselves in sorrow before Him the greatest debt of sin, and yet so many hard-hearted people refuse to forgive others the least trifle, the smallest offence. How much enmity is there not even amongst relatives who hate one another so much that if they could, they would ruin one another. In a word, God's mercy is inexhaustible, and yet so many Christians are implacable in their enmity and are destitute of compassion or charity.

Dear Brethren, do not pronounce against yourselves the sentence of condemnation when you pray daily. "Forgive us our trespasses, as we forgive those who trespass against us." "Let not the sun go down upon your anger."

O most merciful God and Savior! we thank Thee for the lesson which Thou hast given us to-day. Help us, poor weak mortals as we are, that we may not regard the greatness of the injury done to us by our enemies, but rather may follow the example which Thou didst give us when dying on the Cross and may learn to pray with Thee "Father forgive them, for they know not what they do." Amen.

TWENTY-SECOND SUNDAY AFTER PENTECOST

Matt. xxii, 15–21

To Each One His Own

> "Render therefore to Cæsar the things that are Cæsar's; and God, the things that are God's."
>
> Matt. xxii, 21.

DEAR BRETHREN: The incident recorded in to-day's Gospel occurred in the last days of our Lord's Life just before His Passion. The impious Pharisees, who had determined on His death, wanted to entrap Him by an artfully contrived question. But they themselves fell into the trap. The Proverb says: "He who digs a pit for another, falls into it himself." Let us listen to the account.

I. "RENDER TO CÆSAR WHAT BELONGS TO CÆSAR"

Our Lord's enemies had put to Him the cunningly-devised question, "Is it lawful to give tribute to Cæsar or not?" If our Lord had answered: yes it was right and they were in duty bound to do so, the Jewish people would have risen against Him, for they were sworn enemies to such taxes. If He had said: No, they would have denounced Him to Pilate for inciting the people to rebel.

Our Lord knew their evil designs, therefore He asked to see one of the Roman coins in which the tribute was paid, and He then inquired: "Whose image and inscription is this?" They were forced to make answer, "Cæsar's." Then said our Lord, "Render therefore, to Cæsar, the things that are Cæsar's, and to God, the things that are God's." The meaning of these words is: Because you are Cæsar's subjects, as your money which he had coined for you and which you use in your business shows, you must indeed easily understand that it is right and reasonable to pay to him the appointed tax, and give back to him the coins which bear his image.

Dear Brethren, this answer holds good for all time and for us.

To obey our earthly rulers is a sacred duty, a divine commandment, as St. Paul taught the early Roman Christians whose Emperor and his officials were heathens.

"Let every soul be subject to higher powers: for there is no power but from God: and those that are, are ordained of God. Therefore he that resisteth the power, resisteth the ordinance of God. And they that resist, purchase to themselves damnation. "Wherefore be subject of necessity, not only for wrath, but also for conscience-sake. For therefore also you pay tribute. For they are the ministers of God, serving unto this purpose. Render therefore to all men their dues. Tribute, to whom tribute is due: custom to whom custom: fear to whom fear: honor to whom honor."

II. AND TO GOD, THE THINGS THAT ARE GOD'S

The little word "and" was used by our Lord to signify that both sayings are quite reconcilable one with the other. Man has a heavenly destiny, but he has also an earthly one and he must fulfil both. But as God, Heaven, and Eternity are of far more importance than Cæsar, the world and Time, so also of far more importance is the second sentence: "Render to God what belongs to God."

Our immortal soul is also a coin upon which is stamped the image of God and which must therefore be given back to Him undefaced, undefiled, as it was consecrated to Him in Baptism.

St. Bernard adduces four reasons why we should devote our souls entirely to God and perform for Him all the duties of our calling.

1. He is our Creator; we are His creatures; He is the Artist; we are the work of His hands. Where is the artist who does not demand the fruit of his labor?

2. We must consecrate ourselves wholly to God because we have fallen away from Him by a lukewarm, sinful life. Our past sins require of us that we should employ the time remaining to us in bringing forth fruits worthy of penance.

3. We can only purchase eternal happiness by giving ourselves entirely to God.

4. A God Man has sacrificed for us His infinitely precious life. Therefore, if we had a thousand lives, we should from gratitude gladly sacrifice them for Him.

Dear Brethren, to-day, make a firm resolution to consecrate yourself wholly to the service of God Who has given Himself first to you; give and devote your intellect to Him by lively faith, your heart by fervent love, your will by submission to His Commandments, your body by subduing evil desires, and by patience in all your sufferings; in a word, direct by a good intention, all your actions to God and offer Him a perfect sacrifice of praise, adoration, and of your everlasting love. Amen.

Twenty-third Sunday after Pentecost

Matt. ix, 18-26

Remembrance of Death

> "Lord, my daughter is even now dead."
>
> Matt. ix, 18.

DEAR BRETHREN: In to-day's Gospel a woman who was afflicted for twelve years with a grievous malady is healed by merely touching the hem of our divine Redeemer's robe, and the ruler's daughter is raised from the dead by the touch of His hand. Let us learn the plain lesson here taught us that we cannot for one moment be secure against sickness and death, and also that the hour of our death will be extremely bitter if we put off thinking of death until the end of our lives.

To-day, therefore, let the remembrance of death come vividly before us, and with Jesus, Peter, James, and John let us enter the death-chamber.

I. WHAT DOES THIS DEAD GIRL PREACH TO US?

1. No age, no position, high or low, is safe from the arrows of death; sooner or later, dear Brethren, you will fall a victim to him; your life hangs, as it were, by a thread which any day or hour may break. Death for us all is absolutely certain; the hour of its coming is alone uncertain.

This dead girl says to us: Work while it is yet day, for the night (which is the hour of death) cometh when no man can any longer work. With every step, you are drawing nearer to the life beyond, and it depends upon yourself whether that life shall be filled with everlasting joys, or be one of eternal misery, according as you lead a good life here below, or spend that life in sin.

We are here to-day, and gone to-morrow.

PENTECOST 211

2. Hence, strive by good works to make your election sure, by the practice of virtue, and the fulfilment of your duties to prepare yourself for a life of eternal happiness. The surest means of this end is the frequent thought of death. "In all thy works remember thy last end, and thou shalt never sin." [1]

If in every action, we remember that perhaps it may be the last act of our lives, that perhaps this very day we must die and appear before God our Judge, surely, this thought will give us strength to resist every temptation to sin. The man who daily remembers death, will not fix his heart on earthly riches which he must soon leave behind, nor on vain, transitory pleasures, nor on the desires of his body which withers like a flower of the field; he looks rather to the riches of Eternity and to the everlasting joys of the future life. Therefore, dear Brethren, in all your works remember the four last things

II. WHAT DOES THIS GIRL LYING ON HER BIER TEACH US?

1. This girl's death was but a brief slumber from which she would be shortly awakened by

---
[1] Ecclesiast. vii, 40.

the divine Redeemer. You also, Brethren, will one day lie without life, pale, still and cold on your bier; then, you will be laid, sleeping the sleep of death, in the grave which will be closed and your friends will say: "He rests in peace," or, "she rests in peace." They will go away and leave you lying there for ever. No father, no mother, no friend will every come to awaken you, to bid you "Arise." And at last when father, mother, brothers, sisters, friends, in their turn also go to rest in "God's Acre," then you will be quite forgotten by men, there will be none to remember you.

But it will not be always thus. A day will come, it may be after long ages. When the Lord will say: "Arise, ye dead!" And then your soul shall return to your body, your heart shall beat once more, and your eyes shall behold your Savior, and His angels shall place you, as we hope and pray, on His right hand where you shall hear those consoling words "Come ye blessed of my Father; possess ye the kingdom which has been prepared for you from the beginning of the world.

This joy, this eternal happiness, shall we all attain if we live according to the teachings of

Jesus Christ, and persevere in faith, hope, and love. Therefore, follow your divine Savior; pay no heed to the votaries of the world who would lead you astray. Remain fixed in faith in Jesus Christ who awakens the dead; animate your hope in Him who never abandons anyone who takes refuge in Him; love Jesus who has given His life for you, that so on the great Resurrection Day, He may awaken you also from sleep, and take you with Him into the Kingdom of His Heavenly Father. Amen.

Twenty-fourth Sunday after Pentecost

Matt. xxiv, 15-35

Eternal Torments or Eternal Life

> "Heaven and earth shall pass away, but my word shall not pass away."
> Matt. xxiv, 35.

Dear Brethren: To-day, the Church unfolds to us our Lord's great prediction concerning the fearful punishments which should overtake the blind and hardened Jews, and which was fulfilled to the letter. But in the fate of this people is foreshadowed our own. *The destruction of Jerusalem is an image of the end of the world.*

Eternal torments or Eternal life is the inconceivable final scene in the world's great drama. Who does not feel the tremendous importance of these words? Should we not our whole life long, but more especially now at the close of the ecclesiastical year, keep constantly before our eyes, that great journey into Eternity which is ever drawing nearer?

Let us ask ourselves, dear Brethren, what are the warnings concerning this last day which our divine Saviour gives us in to-day's Gospel.

I. "FLEE TO THE MOUNTAINS"

Our Lord admonished His disciples to fly from Jerusalem as soon as they should see the signs and presages of the approaching devastation. The early Christians, therefore, quitted house and lands to save the life of their bodies. What shall we do to secure the salvation of our immortal souls?

Ah! how little do we sacrifice for this end. In holy Scripture there is nothing so strongly impressed on us as to fly from those persons and those places which might lead us into sin. "Flee ye from the midst of Babylon, and let every one save his own life: be not silent upon her iniquity: for it is the time of revenge from the Lord, he will render unto her what she hath deserved."[1] "Fly fornication."[2] "Flee from sins as from the face of a serpent: for if thou comest near them, they will take hold of thee. The teeth thereof are the teeth of a lion, killing the souls of men."[3]

Our divine Savior also commands us to part with all those things which endanger our salvation, no matter how precious or how necessary to us they may be. "It is better for thee having one eye to enter into life, than having two eyes to be cast into hell fire."[4]

Ah! how many men persist in incurring the danger of eternal damnation, just for the sake of momentary pleasure, or of a trifling gain, or from human respect. Dear Brethren, pray with King David, "I have lifted up my eyes to the mountains, from whence help shall come to me. My help is from the Lord, who made heaven and earth."[5]

II. BELIEVE NOT THE FALSE PROPHETS

"For there will rise up false Christs and false prophets, and they shall shew signs and wonders,

---

[1] Jer. li, 6.   [2] I Cor. vi, 18.   [3] Eccles. xxi, 2.
[4] Matt. xviii, 9.   [5] Ps. cxx, 1, 2.

to seduce (if it were possible) even the elect. Take you heed therefore."[1]

Such is the warning which is given to us by the Son of God. In those days, in Jerusalem, were to be found many deceivers who represented themselves as the true Messiah and as benefactors of the people, and thus enticed the credulous to their destruction. And, equally, in the present day, godless men similarly deceive the people, crying out: "Away with the old Christianity! We want to enlighten you and to make you happy." And they find many to follow them because of their catchword: Away from Rome! Religion is a matter of individual opinion. And they gain still more approval because they lead the deluded people into sensuality, licentiousness and anarchy, and promise them out of all this happiness and prosperity.

Do not be deceived, do not believe these men who deny God. The Apostle St. Jude in a sermon wherein he threatened such men with fearful punishment warned the early Christians against them: " For certain men are secretly entered in (who were written of long ago unto this judgment), ungodly men, turning the grace of our Lord God

---

[1] Mark xiv, 22, 23.

into riotousness, and denying the only sovereign Ruler, and our Lord, Jesus Christ. As Sodom and Gomorrah, and the neighboring cities, in like manner, having given themselves to fornification, and going after other flesh, were made an example, suffering the punishment of eternal fire. In like manner these men also defile the flesh, and despise dominion, and blaspheme majesty." [1]

Frightful indeed is the mere thought of God's eternal justice. Well might the whole human race make lamentation because of it. O! never fraternise with impious blasphemers, but implore of your Crucified Redeemer grace and mercy now and at the hour of your death. Amen

---

[1] Jude i, 7–13.

PART SECOND

FEASTS OF THE ECCLESIASTICAL YEAR

FEASTS OF OUR LORD JESUS CHRIST

FEAST OF THE NATIVITY OF CHRIST
(CHRISTMAS DAY)

Luke ii, 1–14

The Crib at Bethlehem

> "And the Word was made flesh, and dwelt amongst us."
> John i, 14.

DEAR BRETHREN: To-day we celebrate the great Feast for which during the four weeks of Advent we have been preparing. On this day the Son of the Eternal Father for our salvation came down from Heaven and was born in a stable at Bethlehem. "The Word was made flesh, and dwelt amongst us." Hence, let us join in the glorious canticle of the Angels who sang "Glory be to God in the highest, and on earth peace to men of good will."

What are the lessons which we learn from the divine Infant Jesus in His Crib?

I. BEFORE HIS BIRTH

1. The Roman Emperor Augustus ordered a census to be taken of all his subjects that he might know how many soldiers he could levy, and what taxes he could impose. Augustus was a pagan Emperor, yet, Joseph with Mary obeyed the order to go to Bethlehem there to inscribe their names, although to do so entailed on them much hardship.

We too, dear Brethren, must obey our lawful rulers in all that is not against our conscience. We must not insult those in authority nor exaggerate their faults; nor must we try to lower them in the esteem and respect of others.

The Prophet Micheas had predicted [1] that the Savior of the world should be born in Bethlehem. " And thou, Bethlehem Ephrata, art a little one among the thousands of Juda: out of thee shall he come forth unto me that is to be the ruler in Israel: and his going forth is from the beginning, from the days of eternity."

A pagan emperor was the instrument for the fulfilment of this prophecy, and by his edict obliged Mary and Joseph to journey to Bethle-

---
[1] v, 2.

hem where Jesus was born. Instead of regarding this proclamation as a misfortune, they looked upon it as a secret dispensation of God. So too, dear Brethren, should you be resolved to accept the hardest fate in this spirit of resignation, and to await the end patiently. Leave all things to divine Providence, for to those whom God loves all things work unto good.

II. AT HIS BIRTH

1. As in the whole of the little town of Bethlehem no shelter for the night could be found, Joseph with Mary was obliged to seek shelter in a cave in which cattle were housed. This miserable stable was the palace in which the King of heaven and earth willed to make His first appearance on earth. Thus in the very moment of His birth He gave us the example of those virtues which later He was to teach us by word as well as example, humility, self-denial, and love of the Cross. Jesus would correct in men their predominant failings which led them to value earthly riches, honors and pleasures more than virtue. If He had come on earth in splendour and luxury, then would His Sermon on the Mount, in which He pronounced blessed

the poor, the humble, the mourner, those who suffer persecution for justice sake, have made little or no impression. By word and example, our Lord shows us that in His Kingdom nothing is of value save virtue and holiness.

2. And what does the divine Infant lying on the cold hard straw preach to us? O children of men! He seems to say, look upon sin as the greatest evil in this world; I weep bitter tears because of the sins of men for which I have undertaken to atone. If the Eternal Father, because of the sins of others chastises so severely His only Begotten Son, how will He deal with those proud, audacious sinners themselves?

III. AFTER THE BIRTH OF OUR LORD

1. An angel having announced to them the glad tidings of our Savior's birth, the shepherds hastened to the Crib where falling on their knees, they humbly adored the divine Child. Almighty God indeed favors the lowliest among men. The Angel did not appear to the well-to-do inhabitants of Bethlehem who were living in ease and comfort.

Dear Brethren, strive to be as free from sin and as pleasing to God as the lowly shepherds.

Pray to the divine Child in His Crib that He may inflame your hearts with His love, for Jesus is love itself, and to love Jesus and to be loved by Him is Heaven's own bliss.

Like the poor shepherds, the Angelic choirs made amends for the ingratitude of mankind, and sang their glorious canticles of praise to the new-born Redeemer.

Let us join these Angelic spirits in their sublime " Gloria."

"Glory be to God on high," Glory be to the Father Who has sent to us His divine Son that we the lost children of Adam might become His children; Glory be to the Son Who has taken away the sins of the world and has opened to us the gates of Heaven which had been closed against us; Glory be to the Holy Ghost the Father of the poor, the Giver of all good things; may He fill our hearts with His divine love and grant the peace of Heaven to all on earth who are of good will. Amen.

Feast of the Circumcision

(NEW YEAR'S DAY)

Luke ii, 21

The Value of Time

> "And the Angel . . . swore . . . That time shall be no longer." Apoc. x, 5, 6.

DEAR BRETHREN: On this the eighth day after the joyful birth of the divine Infant, according to the Law of Moses He was circumcised, and received the name of Jesus which signifies Redeemer and Savior, this name being given to Him because He was come to redeem men from sin and to restore to them salvation and the grace of God and the hope of eternal happiness.

But we must, ourselves, co-operate in this work of our salvation, therefore let us spend the New Year well by keeping the Commandments of God, and by following the example of Jesus Christ, for the time of our mortal life is short and precious.

I. THE DAYS OF OUR LIFE ARE FEW

1. Time flies quickly; men come and go; all things earthly last indeed but a moment as

it were. "Man born of a woman, living for a short time, is filled with many miseries. Who cometh forth like a flower, and is destroyed, and fleeth as a shadow, and never continueth in the same state." [1]

My Brethren: do not labor so hard to procure for yourself the brief pleasures of this mortal life. Ah! What does it profit a man if he gain the whole world and suffer the loss of his own soul?

In the mysterious Apocalypse,[2] we read that John, the beloved Disciple, saw an Angel of God who with hand uplifted to Heaven swore by Him that liveth for ever and ever, Who created Heaven and earth, that great oath, so fraught with meaning "That time shall be no longer." Thus, therefore, all things shall pass away. No longer will hours lengthen into days, days glide into weeks, weeks into months, months into years, in ever changing succession and return. All will be at an end. Nothing will remain save God and Eternity; all earthly activity will cease.

As the tree falls so does it lie, to the right or to the left. Once we have reached the end of

---
[1] Job xiv, 1, 2. [2] Apoc. x, 5, 6.

our allotted days, we shall, ah! perhaps too late, cry out with Solomon, "Vanity of vanities, and all is vanity."

Therefore, let us watch and pray. Let us do good whilst there is yet time, before we are overtaken by the night. Let us act prudently like wise men, not like fools. "Remember thy Creator in the days of thy youth, before the time of affliction come, and the years draw nigh of which thou shalt say: They please me not." [1]

Now, at the beginning of the New Year the Apostle admonishes us that "it is now the hour for us to rise from sleep. For now our salvation is nearer than when we believed." [2] Solemn, thrilling thought: Life is but a brief dream; Eternity knows no end. How is it with your soul? Ask yourself this question seriously.

II. TIME IS PRECIOUS

Almighty God in His infinite Mercy has bestowed on man many gifts and graces, but of them all time is the most precious. Time is that pearl spoken of in the Gospel, for which men must give up everything that with it they may obtain the treasure of eternal life.

---

[1] Eccles. xii, 1. [2] Rom. xiii, 11.

The Heavenly Father has planted a vineyard which His divine Son has fructified with His Precious Blood, and which the Holy Ghost by means of His grace causes to flourish. Before this vineyard we stand in the market place of life, and at every hour of the day the call of God comes to us; why stand you idle there? Go into my vineyard, labor and exert yourself to bring forth fruit before the day draws to a close. Time is short and the Bridegroom stands at the gate; soon, soon, and when we least expect it, He will enter into the heavenly Marriage Feast, and only those who during this brief time of their mortal lives, have filled the lamp of faith with the oil of good works, will go with Jesus into the kingdom of the Heavenly Father where all good things have been prepared from the beginning. Amen.

FEAST OF THE EPIPHANY

Adoration of the Magi

Matt. ii, 1–12

Gold, Frankincense and Myrrh

> "They offered him gifts; gold, frankincense, and myrrh."
> Matt. ii, 11.

Dear Brethren: To-day Jesus Christ appeared to the Gentiles in His divinity and in His human nature.

Let us now consider the Adoration of the three Kings according to the picture drawn for us in the Gospel.

I. FALLING DOWN THEY ADORED THE DIVINE CHILD

1. After the three Wise Men had taken leave of Herod in Jerusalem, guided by the Star they went to Bethlehem where they found the Child with Mary His Mother, and falling down they adored Him.

Divinely enlightened, they recognized hidden in the Child the divine Majesty. God had enlightened them exteriorly by the miraculous star and interiorly by the Holy Ghost. Oh! what a beautiful example of reverence and devotion to our Redeemer is given to us by these three Wise Men. Princes of high rank as they were, they did not hesitate to fall prostrate before a helpless infant. Our Faith teaches us that the same Jesus, who was born at Bethlehem, still remains night and day in our churches that He may bestow His favors on all those who implore them with humility and confidence. How these three Kings put to shame the irreverence of so many Catholics who enter the House of God with a proud demeanor and in unbecoming dress, as if they would have themselves admired and adored as idols. What a strict account they will have to render to the divine Judge for talking and laughing in the Church, and looking all round them rather than at Jesus on the Altar.

"But if any man violate the temple of God; him shall God destroy." [1] Remember, my Brethren, the words of the great Apostle: [2] "That in the name of Jesus every knee should bow, of those that are in heaven, on earth, and under the earth:"

---

[1] Cor. iii, 17.   [2] Philipp. ii, 10.

II. THEY OFFERED THE CHILD GOLD, FRANKINCENSE AND MYRRH

1. These three gifts beautifully express the dignity of the divine Child; as to a king they offer Him gold, as God, frankincense, and as man, myrrh. Thus was fulfilled what the Prophet Isaias had foretold six hundred years before: " All they from Saba shall come, bringing gold and frankincense: and shewing forth praise to the Lord." [3]

Jesus requires gifts from us also. We offer our Lord gold, when from supernatural motives we love God and our neighbor. Love is the most precious of all virtues, as gold is the most precious of all metals. Again, we offer Him gold when we, according to our means, help in the adornment of our churches and assist the poor by our alms, for what we do to the least of our brethren we do to Jesus Christ Himself.

We offer our Lord frankincense when we acknowledge Him as our God and in deepest humility adore Him; when we devoutly assist at the Holy Sacrifice of the Mass; when with pious preparation we receive the Sacraments and often during the day lift up our hearts to

---
[3] Is. lx, 6.

God, for prayer ascends like incense to the Throne of God.

You bring as a gift to Jesus the bitter myrrh, when from love of Him you keep watch over your eyes and restrain your tongue; when you suppress your anger, your pride and all evil thoughts and desires; when you shun all disgraceful pleasures or works and when you bear all troubles and contradictions which God sends you, patiently for love of Jesus. You offer Him myrrh when you take care that the dying receive the last Sacraments and when you pray for the suffering souls in Purgatory. Dear Brethren, let us thank the Heavenly Father for having revealed to us His divine Son as He did to the Wise Men, and let us imitate these holy Kings in faith and good works that we may one day with them behold Jesus face to face in His eternal Glory. Amen.

FEAST OF THE MOST HOLY NAME OF JESUS
Luke ii, 11
A Name above All Names

> "God . . . hath given him a name which is above all names." Philipp. ii, 9.

DEAR BRETHREN: The Church, to-day celebrates the great Feast of the divine Name of

Jesus whose Almighty Power was made manifest, as recorded in the Gospel, at the marriage feast of Cana.

Mary, the Mother of Jesus, said to her Son, "They have no wine" and turning, she spoke to the attendants, saying: "Whatsoever he shall say to you, do ye." And our Lord commanded them: "Fill up the waterpots with water." And when the chief steward tasted this fresh wine, he found it was far better than what had been served at first.

His heavenly Father has given our divine Lord a name which is above all names.

I. AN ALL-POWERFUL NAME

1. St. Bernard speaking of this Holy Name, says very beautifully: "When I think of the Name of Jesus, I represent to myself the divine Savior as He sits at the right hand of the Father, possessing all power in Heaven and earth, I represent to myself Jesus the most Beautiful, the most Amiable, Who is our Mediator in Heaven and Who has power to send us help if we call upon His name with reverence and devotion."[1]

Jesus foretold to His disciples what wonders

---
[1] Serm. in Cant.

should be wrought in His Name: " In my name they shall cast out devils: they shall speak with new tongues. They shall take up serpents; and if they shall drink any deadly thing, it shall not hurt them: they shall lay their hands upon the sick, and they shall recover."[1]

At the gate of the Temple in Jerusalem which was called the Gate Beautiful, there sat every day a man who was lame from his birth, and who asked alms from all that passed by. Peter and John happened one day to pass this man as they were going into the Temple and he asked of them an alms, whereupon, Peter said to him: " Silver and gold I have none; but what I have, I give thee: In the name of Jesus Christ of Nazareth, arise, and walk." And instantly the cripple was cured. He stood up, leaping with joy and praising God in a loud voice. All the people witnessed this miracle, and gave praise to the Name of Jesus.

Let us praise the Almighty Power of the divine Name of Jesus; let us invoke this most holy Name in all our needs, our troubles, in all spiritual and temporal afflictions. O divine Jesus! have mercy on me:

---

[1] Mark xvi, 17, 18.

II. A HOLY NAME

1. This Name of Jesus was given to the Savior of the world not by man, but by the Heavenly Father Himself. The Archangel announced to Mary: "Thou shalt call his name Jesus."

Hence the Church ever pronounces this most Holy Name with the most profound and adoring reverence, and the priest as often as he names it, uncovers and bows his head.

Dear Brethren, do you wish to be delivered from your sins, and to obtain grace and mercy from God; then cry out from the depths of your soul, "My Jesus! mercy." In all temptations make use of this most powerful weapon of defence. "For there is no other name under heaven given to men whereby we must be saved." [1]

Let us listen to St. Bernard who exhorts us. "If anyone is sad, let but the Name of Jesus arise from his heart to his lips and all his melancholy will vanish; his soul will regain peace, and heavenly serenity will fill his heart and spirit; if anyone has committed a crime, and in his despair would with his own hand take away his life, the instant that he invokes this life-giving

---

[1] iv, 12.

Name, all the terrifying phantoms of Hell are banished and he begins to live again. There is no passion the wild assaults of which will not be repulsed by this most holy Name." [1]

Dear Brethren, in every circumstance of life, remember that the strength of the all-powerful, and most Holy Name of Jesus will give you consolation and help. Invoke it, not in malediction, nor in rage and hatred, but with profoundest reverence and ardent love for Jesus. Strive so to live that in every need you may be worthy of the assistance of God made Man, Jesus Christ, and thus secure your eternal salvation. Amen.

Monday in Easter Week

Luke xxiv, 13–35

Jesus Our Companion Through Life

> "And it came to pass, that while they talked and reasoned with themselves, Jesus himself also drawing near went with them." Luke xxiv, 15.

Dear Brethren: After His glorious Resurrection from the dead, our divine Lord repeatedly appeared to His disciples; He strengthened their faith in His Divinity, and invested Saint

---

[1] Sermo. 15 in cant.

Peter with supreme authority as Head of His Church on earth. "Feed my lambs; feed my sheep."

On this the second day after His Resurrection our Lord appeared to two of the disciples on the road to Emmaus, and accompanied them on their journey, enlightening them as to the manner in which the Scriptures had been fulfilled in His Passion and Death. He went with them to the inn, and as He blessed the bread and gave it to them to eat, their eyes were opened and they recognised their Lord.

We, also, dear Brethren, are travellers, pilgrims journeying to Eternity. O may our divine Savior go with us on our way, that thus in His company, we may attain to the goal of our journey: a happy Eternity.

What do we receive from our divine Savior as He journeys with us on our pilgrimage? He ministers to us as He did to the disciples at Emmaus:

1. *A Mild Reproof.* The two disciples were unable to reconcile the sublime dignity of the Messias with the mournful events of His Passion and Death, and thus they became involved in doubt and darkness and their faith wavered.

Our Lord, therefore, gently rebuked them, but this rebuke was not so much a reproach as the expression of the love of His divine Heart, and He enlightened them regarding the mystery of the Redemption.

Learn from this to admonish an erring brother gently and in private, not before others. If he will listen to you, you have won him to God.[1]

If we have reason to hope that our erring neighbor will amend his ways, then we are in conscience bound to admonish him as our brother, and to pray that he may forsake his wrong-doing. To flatter the sinner and cold-bloodedly to let him slumber in his sins; that is cruelty.

If a man wanted to drown himself, we should try to prevent him. How much more then should we try to restrain those who by their sins are plunging into Hell.

2. *Sweet Consolation in Suffering.* "Ought not Christ to have suffered these things, and so to enter into his glory?"[2] Jesus had indeed, of His own free will, suffered all that He willed to suffer, as He Himself declared. "No man taketh it [His life] away from me; but I lay it down

---

[1] Matth. xviii, 15.   [2] Luke, xxiv, 26.

of myself." [1] He had only to suffer in so far as to become the Redeemer of the sinful lost human race, to accomplish the Will of His Heavenly Father, and to fulfil the predictions of the Prophets.

Dear Brethren, in these words what sweet consolation has our divine Savior given us for all the trials and sufferings which our heavenly Father sends us. Of what avail is all our murmuring, all our complaining, which only serves to make our trials greater and to increase our guilt?

To suffer, to endure, daily to fight against our evil inclinations, to accept all the contradictions of this life and death itself: such is the way to Eternal Life, the gate by which we enter into glory, the key which unlocks to us everlasting joys.

But alas! many object to hearing anything about suffering; they would fain know nothing but unbroken happiness; they want to have Heaven here and hereafter. Those who wish to suffer nothing are looking for another way to Eternal Glory than that trodden by Jesus. Only when we suffer, are we "heirs indeed of God, and joint heirs with Christ; yet so, if we

---
[1] John x, 18.

suffer with him, that we may be also glorified with him."[1]

Our Lord also gives us on our pilgrimage, as He did to the disciples at Emmaus.

3. Holy Communion: " And it came to pass, whilst he was at table with them, he took bread, and blessed and brake, and gave to them. And their eyes were opened, and they knew him."

O those blessed moments of Holy Communion! every day this happiness may be ours, if we only have a holy longing for Jesus, and prepare our souls to receive this divine Guest. Strengthened by this Heavenly Food, we shall joyfully continue our earthly pilgrimage to its blessed end. Our eyes too shall be opened; we shall grow ever more and more in the knowledge and love of Jesus until, one day, we shall behold Him face to face and shall love Him for all Eternity. Amen.

---

[1] Rom. viii, 17

Feast of the Ascension

Mark xvi, 14–20

Until We Meet in Heaven

> "And the Lord Jesus, after he had spoken to them, was taken up into heaven, and sitteth on the right hand of God." Mark xvi, 19.

DEAR BRETHREN: Our Lord on the fortieth day after His Resurrection from the dead, assembled His disciples in Jerusalem, and after having partaken of a repast with them He led them to the Mount of Olives and there before their eyes ascended into Heaven.

As they stood, their longing gaze fixed upon the heavens into which their divine Master had vanished from sight, there appeared beside them two angels in white garments who said to them: " Ye men of Galilee, why stand you looking up to heaven? This Jesus who is taken up from you into heaven, shall so come, as you have seen him going into heaven." [1]

Let us, to-day, take our stand beside these happy disciples and learn from them;

1. *That We Too Must Look Upwards after*

---

[1] Acts i, 11.

Jesus. Our regards must ever be fixed on Heaven; yonder is our true home whither Jesus has gone before us to prepare for us a dwelling and to be our Mediator with His Heavenly Father. On this day of His Ascension into Heaven where He "sitteth on the right hand of God," Jesus Christ, true Man as well as true God, by raising our human nature united to His Divinity over all the angels to the right hand of the Father has thus restored to it the high dignity which it possessed in the Garden of Eden before Adam's fall.

In the words of the Apostle. "Where sin abounded, grace did more abound." [1]

In Heaven we shall meet again. "Therefore, if you be risen with Christ, seek the things that are above, where Christ is sitting at the right hand of God: Mind the things that are above, not the things that are upon the earth." [2]

Daily from the Altar the Church calls upon us to lift our hearts to Heaven: "Sursum Corda!" "Lift up your hearts!" And she constantly exhorts us to think frequently of Heaven. Truly there is scarcely any thought so calculated to urge us to do good and to avoid evil, to give us

---
[1] Rom. v, 20.   [2] Colos. iii, 1, 2.

courage in suffering and temptation as this thought of Heaven.

2. *We Should Adore Jesus Christ.* To Jesus Christ who sits at the right hand of His Father all power is given in Heaven and on earth. He is our Sovereign Lord and the invisible Head and Bridegroom of the Church; He is our All in all. Let us adore Him. Let us offer to Him in the most Holy Sacrament of the Altar our lowliest adoration.

3. *We Must Look Forward to the Second Coming of Our Lord on the Day of Judgment.* " This Jesus Who is taken up from you into Heaven, shall so come, as you have seen him going into heaven," said the angels to the disciples.

The enemy of our salvation strives to prevent us thinking of the Last Judgment that thus we may forget how inexorable is divine Justice and so fall into sin.

Let us ever pray: " O Jesus! be to me not a judge but a Savior."

4. We must return to whatever calling God has appointed to us in life, and faithfully and cheerfully fulfil those duties which are allotted to us. You are not called to preach from the pulpit, but you must preach to others by your

example, by your Christian life, that thus Jesus Christ may be ever more and more known, loved and honored.

Dear Brethren, we must labor diligently for the salvation of our souls. Saint Augustine says: "Our pride cannot soar into Heaven, for Heaven is the kingdom of the humble. The avaricious man cannot ascend there, because to gain the most precious treasures of the Kingdom of Heaven we must count all the riches of this world as nothing; impurity cannot enter there, for only the pure of heart shall see God."

Heaven is our Home. In Heaven eternal riches shall be ours; in Heaven everlasting happiness awaits us. May we all meet in Heaven. Amen.

Whit-Monday

John iii, 16–21

The Excess of Divine Love

> "For God so loved the world as to give his only begotten Son." John iii, 16.

DEAR BRETHREN: These words in to-day's Gospel which were spoken by our divine Savior to Nicodemus are the basis on which rest our faith, our everlasting hope and our love.

Come, O Holy Ghost! teach us to comprehend this mystery rightly that thus we may be saved.

In these words we recognise:

I. THE EXCESS OF DIVINE LOVE

1. "*God So Loved the World.*" Yes; only infinite love could have caused the Eternal Father to send His only begotten Son into the world, for God is in Himself eternally happy and needs not man's praise or worship. Before Him all nations are as a drop of water, and the islands as a little dust.[1]

2. "*So Loved the World.*" Not a grateful world worthy of His love, but a sin-stained world, filled with abominations, a world which knew not God, which sought Him not, a world which ever and always offended Him.

3. "*His Only Begotten Son.*" If God had given to us all the angelic choirs what would they have been in comparison to His only Son. If a son, an only son, is to an earthly father so infinitely precious, an object of such tender love, what must be His Co-equal Son to the Eternal Father? Hence God could give us no greater proof of His love nor could He give us any

---

[1] Rom. viii, 32.

greater gift. "How hath he not also, with him, given us all things?"

"*Given to Us.*" Wholly, unreservedly. Jesus is wholly ours: His life, His labors and weariness; His prayers and tears; His precious Blood, His sacred wounds; His Passion and Death.

Never yet has it been heard that a king commanded his only son to lay aside his royal rank, to lead a long, laborious life, and then to die at the hands of wicked rebellious subjects. What men have never done nor never will do, the Heavenly Father has done. For His enemies, for us sinners, He has given His only Son that the gates of Heaven might be reopened to us.

II. THE FULNESS OF THE PROFFERED SALVATION

"*That Whosoever Believeth in Him, May not Perish, but May Have Life Everlasting.*"

1. Dear Brethren, behold God's loving design. He wills to save all; He is concerned that none should be lost; He knows the greatness of the misery into which by sin we should precipitate ourselves. Then, outraged love makes advances to the offenders, anticipates them and pays an infinite price to save them that they may have Eternal Life.

2. *And What are the Conditions on our Part?* *"That We Believe in Him,"* and confess this faith by our lives and our love for God and our neighbor. Dear Brethren, to what should this divine love urge us? Love calls for a return of love. The Beloved Disciple says to us: "Let us therefore love God because God first hath loved us . . . and sent His Son to be a propitiation for our sins." [1]

How many men have little or no love for God; to think of Him even in the church, to pray to Him, hear His divine Word, approach the Sacraments: to such men, all this is intolerable. Their only delight is in gambling, wanton amusements, immodest conversations. They strive but to satisfy the desires of the flesh, to please a sinful world which is ever and always the enemy of God.

"Love not the world," my Brethren, "nor the things which are in the world. If any man love the world, the charity of the Father is not in him." [2]

Give your heart and your love wholly to Almighty God Who has so loved you that He gave His only begotten Son to save you from eternal destruction. Amen.

---

[1] John iv, 10, 19.   [2] John ii, 15.

Feast of the Dedication of Churches

Luke xix, 1–10

All Salvation is in Jesus

> "This day is salvation come to this house."
> Luke xix, 10.

DEAR BRETHREN: Not to the house of Zaccheus alone has the coming of Jesus Christ brought salvation, but to all consecrated Catholic churches. For Jesus Christ has chosen these churches as His dwelling place where day and night He is ever present in the Adorable Sacrament of the Altar, and where He dispenses great, aye the greatest, graces.

Eternal praise and thanksgiving be to the Lord for having set up His Throne of grace in our midst where He is ever ready to hear our prayers.

To-day let us learn from Zaccheus how salvation may come to us with the coming of Jesus Christ.

DESIRE OF HIS COMING

Zaccheus had the greatest longing to see Jesus and to know Him. Being of very low stature he ran before the crowd and climbed into a tree that he might see Him.

Oh! that you also, my Brethren, might have

as great a longing as Zaccheus had for Jesus and for His churches where, day and night, He waits to give us help and consolation in all our troubles. When you hear the church-bell ringing, say to yourselves: "Jesus is calling me, I must go to His House."

If the Christians of the first three hundred years could return to earth and see our beautiful churches, how astonished they would be; how they would cry out to us: "Oh, Brethren, how happy you are! We were obliged to retire into subterranean cemeteries to assist at Divine Worship; you can assemble in the churches without fear of the executioner's slaves to adore Jesus Christ, to assist at the Divine Mysteries in the Sacrifice of the Mass, and to receive Holy Communion." Even at the present day, what a long distance many Catholics have to journey to reach their remote parish-church.

How beautifully the holy King David expresses the longing desire which we should have for the House of God. "How lovely are thy tabernacles, O Lord of hosts! my soul longeth and fainteth for the courts of the Lord. My heart and my flesh have rejoiced in the living God. For the sparrow hath found herself a house, and the turtle a nest for herself where she may lay her young ones: Thy altars, O Lord of hosts, my king and my God. Blessed are they that dwell in thy house, O Lord: they shall praise thee for ever and ever." [1]

II. JESUS ENTERS INTO OUR HOUSE

Jesus looked up and called Zaccheus by name: "Zaccheus," He said to him, "make haste and come down: for this day I must abide in thy house." And Zaccheus came down quickly "and received him with joy."

To every sinner Jesus says: Come down from the wild fig-tree of your pride, of your sinful habits, of your blind self-love. Purify your soul in the Sacrament of Penance that I may ever abide in your heart. You have indeed heard these words of our Lord oftener than Zaccheus, sometimes spoken by the priest, sometimes by good parents, good friends, sometimes by the voice of conscience. My Brethren, confess your sins often, the oftener the better. Contrite confession is the best means of purifying your souls from sin, of preserving you from grievous sin and

---

[1] Ps. lxxxiii, 2–5.

of preparing you to receive our Lord worthily in Holy Communion. See the wonderful results of the entrance of Jesus into the house of Zaccheus, who from being wholly devoted to money-getting, became instantly as if changed into another being, full of love for his neighbor; he divided half of his wealth amongst the poor and made four-fold restitution to those whom he had wronged. Hitherto money had been his god, his greatest delight; now God alone was his most dearly cherished possession, and to secure his salvation was of more importance to him than all the riches of this world.

Dear Brethren, in you also God's grace through the coming of Jesus will have the most blessed effect both when you receive our Lord in Holy Communion, and when you come to visit Him in the Tabernacle. Oh! visit Jesus in the most holy Sacrament of the Altar as often as you can, even during the week, whenever you pass a church; above all visit Him when He is being offered in the Adorable Sacrifice of the Mass when He offers Himself for you to His Eternal Father.

Thus each time you visit Him, those blessed words of the Lord will be fulfilled in you: "This day is salvation come to this house." Amen.

FEASTS OF THE BLESSED VIRGIN

Feast of the Immaculate Conception

Luke i, 26-28

Mary our New Paradise

> "Thou art all fair, O my love, and there is not a spot in thee." Cant. iv, 7.

DEAR BRETHREN: In the beginning Almighty God planted that garden of delights, Paradise, and placed man therein. But the serpent entered into Paradise and infected Adam and Eve with the poison of sin, and so brought death to the whole human race.

But in Mary God has created for us a new Paradise wherein He placed the second Adam, Jesus Christ, Who has redeemed us all from sin and death, and opened to us the gate which had been closed against us. And the gate of this Paradise, is, as it were, the holy Immaculate Heart of Mary.

Let us enter this Garden of lilies: To-day, the Church calls upon us to honor God's Immaculate Mother of whom the Holy Ghost says: "Thou art all fair, O my love, and there is not a spot in thee." Thus shall we all regain the lost Paradise—here on earth and in Heaven.

I. ON EARTH

1. From all eternity God had chosen the Blessed Virgin to be the Mother, when the time came, of His only begotten Son. Therefore it was fitting that she of whom the All-holy God was to take flesh should never be under Satan's dominion, but should be wholly free from both original and actual sin, immaculately pure and stainless. This the Almighty Power of God could effect, and therefore was it His marvellous act. Already foretold in the Old Covenant as the woman who should crush the serpent's head, praised by the Prophets as the fairest Spouse of the Holy Ghost, the lily without stain, the rose without thorns, the Church has in all ages ever venerated Mary as the Immaculate Virgin Mother of God, and in the year, 1854, she was solemnly proclaimed as such by Pope Pius IX.

Dear Brethren, the children of so pure a Mother must be pure also. If we would rejoice with Mary for ever in Paradise, we must purify ourselves here on earth from sin, and by virtue and purity prepare our hearts for the day when we must leave this world. Hence, the Immaculate Virgin exhorts us: "Come, my children and hear me, I will teach you the fear of the Lord."

Yes: Fear to offend God. Anything on earth rather than commit a mortal sin. It is a question of being a child of Mary or a slave of Satan.

Those who live in God's grace, have peace in their hearts; they have Paradise on earth. And they will also have it in Heaven.

II. IN HEAVEN

"Blessed are the pure in heart, for they shall see God." To help us in attaining to this Heavenly purity and in preserving it, is the office of the Immaculate Virgin whose tender heart is at all times open to us, and in which we can ever find shelter.

Never yet has it been heard and never will, that anyone, even the greatest sinner, who sought refuge in Mary's protection and implored her help, was abandoned by her, and was lost eternally.

Therefore, dear Brethren, joyfully seek refuge with Mary.

FEASTS OF THE BLESSED VIRGIN 253

1. *By Your Interior Veneration.* Whilst you thank God for the extraordinary privilege of her Immaculate Conception, rejoice with Mary for this glorious privilege accorded to her and fervently implore of her to obtain for you from God a pure heart.

2. *By Your External Veneration:* In honor of Mary wear a medal of the Immaculate Conception as a perpetual reminder of your Heavenly Mother. Often during the day salute Mary by devoutly saying the Hail Mary. She will return your salutation; she will defend you in every temptation, and will obtain for you countless graces. Often repeat the indulgenced prayer "Through thy sacred virginity and Immaculate Conception, O Most Blessed Virgin! obtain for me purity of soul and body." On all our Lady's principal Feasts go to Confession and Holy Communion in honor of her Immaculate Conception and unite yourself closely with the most Holy Heart of Mary in praying for the conversion of sinners.

All that you do for the honor of God's Immaculate Mother will be blessed here on earth, and eternally rewarded in Heaven, for Mary will not be outdone by us in love.

Feast of the Purification
(CANDLEMAS DAY)
Luke ii, 22–32

"Mary Offers Her Divine Son in the Temple"

> "They carried him to Jerusalem, to present him to the Lord." Luke ii, 22.

DEAR BRETHREN: On this day Mary and Joseph carried the divine Child to the Temple in Jerusalem to offer Him to the Eternal Father as a Victim for the sins of the world. To-day, therefore, we celebrate the mystery of which we are reminded when we say in the Rosary "Blessed is the fruit of thy womb, Jesus." What special lesson can we draw from this? That we must offer the sacrifice of our life, and at the same time, this mystery affords us consolation for the hour of death.

I. THE OFFERING OF OUR LIFE

Not only did Mary offer her divine Son, but Jesus also offered Himself to His Eternal Father as a victim of atonement, to shed the last drop of His Precious Blood for the Redemption of man, and by His Passion and Death to render infinite satisfaction to the divine Justice so infinitely wronged by the sins of mankind.

Therefore He said to His Father: The sacrifice offered to Thee in the Temple could not please Thee nor atone to Thee sufficiently for the sins of men. Therefore hast Thou fitted a body to Me that I might take the place of these sacrifices.[1]

Dear Brethren, frequently thank your divine Redeemer for having offered His life for love of you; offer to Him in return all the days of your life to be spent in serving and glorifying God, "Glorify and bear God in your body."[2] Offer your eyes to God; turn them away from vanity and sin; often raise them to Heaven. "When I look up to Heaven, how hateful earth seems to me." Offer your tongue to God; only use it in what concerns God's honor and to edify your neighbor. Refrain from cursing, from calumny, and from obscene conversation. Offer your hands to God to labor in the name of Jesus that you may obtain God's blessing. Offer your feet to God as you go to the church. Fly all dangerous amusements and companions. Offer to God your body as the dwelling-place of the Holy Ghost, and let your soul be the altar whence sighs and prayers like sacred flames shall ascend to God.

---

[1] Compare Ps. xxxix, 7–9.   [2] I Cor. vi, 20.

What a beautiful life did Mary offer to God on this day by her deep humility. She was not under any obligation, she who was spotless, to submit to the Jewish purification and to pass in the eyes of all men as an ordinary woman.

What do we learn from this? Mary, the Immaculate Virgin, would gladly hide her privilege and appear less than she is, whilst we are so anxious to appear of more importance than we really are.

Mary who is all-pure fulfils the law of purification, whilst we defiled and sin-stained men trouble so little about sincerely purifying our consciences. Mary did more than she was bound to do. What works of supererogation do we perform? We even cease to perform prescribed works such as fasting, sanctifying the Sunday, until at last, we give up all. And yet, we think we can appease our conscience. In the hour of death shall we be at peace?

II. CONSOLATION WHEN DYING

In the Gospel for to-day's Feast, there appears one who teaches us how to gain true consolation. This happy man, looking forward to his last hour, could pray: " Now dost thou dismiss

Thy servant, O Lord, according to Thy word in peace. Because my eyes have seen Thy salvation."

The holy old man, Simeon, enlightened by the Holy Ghost recognised in the Child Jesus in His mother's arms, the Savior and Redeemer of the world, and he desired now to die that he might take to his forefathers in Limbo the glad tidings of the advent of the Messiah.

Dear Brethren, every time that we receive Jesus into our hearts in Holy Communion, we shall experience the same effects. Things are in a bad way with us, if we have no desire for the kingdom of God, no desire to behold Him glorious in Heaven. We should look upon this world as a place of exile, and cry out with David: "When shall I come and appear before the face of God?" How long shall I continue in danger of losing my eternal salvation? With St. Paul, we should sigh "I long to be dissolved and to be with Christ."

O Lord Jesus Christ, splendor of the Father, Light and consolation of the world, who on this day didst offer Thyself for us to Thy Eternal Father, grant to us through the advocacy of Thy most Holy Mother that we may shun the darkness of sin, may lead a truly virtuous, upright life and may be borne one day, by the hands of angels to the Temple of Thy Eternal Majesty where we shall offer to Thee eternally the sacrifice of praise and thanksgiving. Amen.

Feast of the Annunciation

Luke i, 26–38

The Angelical Salutation

"Hail full of grace the Lord is with thee." Luke i, 28.

Dear Brethren: To-day we celebrate the great Feast of the Incarnation of the Eternal Son of the Heavenly Father in the womb of the Immaculate Virgin Mary.

Three times a day the words which we repeat when saying the Angelus, recall to us this Adorable Mystery. "And the word was made flesh, and dwelt amongst us."

In the Angelical Salutation which we repeat so often in the Rosary we are also reminded of this mystery. "Blessed is the fruit of thy womb Jesus."

Let us consider this salutation first spoken by the Archangel Gabriel to Mary at Nazareth which has been repeated unceasingly throughout the ages and which shall be repeated throughout Eternity.

I. "HAIL MARY"

In whose name does the Angel salute the Immaculate Virgin? The Archangel has been sent by Almighty God Who through His messenger thus Himself salutes Mary.

How exalted the dignity to which God has raised this most pure Virgin when He, Himself, the Lord of Heaven and earth to Whom all creatures are subject thus honors her.

The humble Virgin shunned all observation and remained hidden from the world, accounting herself as the last and least of all. And behold! God makes known her peerless beauty to men and angels.

What does this Salutation import? The import of this Salutation transcends in importance all the most momentous happenings that the world has ever seen. For it portends the Incarnation of the Eternal Son of God, the Redemption of the human race, and the filling up of the places forfeited by the fallen angels. This was the reason why St. Bernard, as he meditated on our Lady's silence when the Angel saluted her, prostrated himself before her, crying out: "O holy Virgin, say Yes: For Heaven, earth, and the souls of the just in Limbo, are waiting on thy answer."

And we pray: O Mary! Refuge of sinners! Thou who for us didst become the Mother of the Redeemer, accept from us also this salutation, and obtain for us that we may be truly converted, may continually amend our lives, and may die a happy death.

II. "FULL OF GRACE"

Mary was conceived full of grace, free from original sin and endowed with countless graces. Grace unceasingly increased in her; her whole life was the purest, holiest service of God, a perpetual advance in the way of perfection.

Observe, dear Brethren, how the Angel in his Salutation did not praise Mary's beauty nor her understanding, although she was the mother of eternal Wisdom, but her fullness of grace. Thus, you should value the grace of God, holiness of soul, far beyond all the riches and glory of this transitory world. Often pray with Saint Ignatius: "O Lord, grant me Thy grace and Thy love, and I am rich enough."

Especially, you, boys and girls, preserve most carefully sanctifying grace which God bestowed on you in Baptism. You were made children of God, and heirs to Heaven.

III. "THE LORD IS WITH THEE"

How wonderful! When the time came, the Eternal Son of God dwelt in Mary, He rested in her womb and afterwards in her arms. He called her Mother and bestowed His infant caresses upon her. For thirty years Jesus, the Lord of Heaven and earth belonged to Mary alone, and was subject to her, for He acknowledged all her rights as a mother. He was present with Mary at the marriage feast of Cana where He worked His first miracle at her request. On the hill of Calvary He committed to John the care of His Mother; after His Resurrection, He appeared to her first and filled her soul with heavenly jubilation. And when Mary was leaving this world, Jesus was with her and took her, soul and body, in triumph to His Kingdom, presented her to the Eternal Father, and placed her at His right Hand on a royal throne that Mary His Mother might be for ever with God, and God with her.

Dear Brethren, when we are seeking the Lord, and sighing for His grace and His help, how shall we find Him more easily than through Mary to whom we can unceasingly say with the Angel Gabriel "the Lord is with thee," and with the Church. "Show unto us the blessed fruit of thy womb Jesus, O clement, O sweet Virgin Mary!"

This is the Angelical Salutation which first uttered in the little room at Nazareth, reechoes throughout the world, is repeated unceasingly by millions of faithful Catholics and which will bring us all consolation, peace, joy, blessing and happiness as long as we live, and Mary's powerful assistance at the hour of our death. Amen.

Feast of the Assumption

Luke x, 38–42

The Best Part

> "Mary hath chosen the best part, which shall not be taken away from her." Luke x, 42.

Dear Brethren: To-day we celebrate the greatest of all the Feasts of God's Blessed Mother, the Feast which is, as it were, the crown and completion of all the other feasts which we celebrate in Mary's honor: the Feast of her Assumption into Heaven.

Of course, you all without exception wish that you too after your death should be taken to Heaven. But mere wishes are of no use. If we desire to be one day with Mary in the glorious Kingdom of God, then, we must now seek the one only thing necessary and choose the best part as our divine Savior tells us in to-day's Gospel. This is the one end and aim of our life, as we must now seriously take to heart. O Mary! pray for us to your divine Son that we may all attain eternal happiness.

1. *"Mary Has Chosen the Best Part which Shall not be Taken Away from her."*

These words were spoken by our divine Lord to Martha, and by them He would seem to say: Martha, the part of looking after the house which you have chosen is certainly a good one, for the affairs of the house must be looked after. But the part which your sister Mary has chosen is the best, for, by hearing the word of God, the soul is strengthened in the principles of Religion, and is encouraged in the practice of virtue whereby Eternal Life is gained.

"Mary has chosen the best part." These words can be applied to no one so well as to the Blessed Virgin. During the whole of her life on earth her greatest joy was to think of God, to serve Him; her only desire was to love Him and to behold Him for ever. This was—notwithstanding her daily household duties which she faithfully performed—her one concern and desire, as it is now her everlasting portion in Heaven whither she was assumed in soul and body. In Heaven Mary is exalted above all the angels and saints because on earth she loved God more than all the blessed Spirits; because she labored more, suffered more, and fought a harder fight.

2. My Brethren: you all desire to share, one day, in Mary's happiness in Heaven. But you must make yourselves deserving of this happiness; you must spare no effort to attain it; you must subdue your passions; you must not allow yourselves to be led into sin; you must labor diligently and unceasingly to grow richer in good works; you must prefer the things of Heaven to those of earth, what is eternal to the fleeting things of this world; the imperishable to the perishable; you must esteem

it a far greater happiness to possess God's grace and friendship than the favor of all mankind.

All men, it is true, wish to die the death of the just—and to go to Heaven. But to wish for the day's wages without having done the day's work; for the victor's laurels without having fought the fight; for a rich harvest without having sowed seed; this is surely an unreasonable wish; this is the disgraceful wish of an idler whom the just God will never reward.

Dear Brethren, as even our best resolutions are weak; as our understanding is filled with darkness and we so often feel a disinclination to good, let us full of confidence, take refuge with Mary who by pleading for us with her divine Son can obtain all things. Never was it heard that a sinner who sought Mary's help was abandoned by her, or lost eternally.

O Mary! Queen of Heaven and of earth, Mother of Mercy, accept us all amongst your servants, and obtain for us from Jesus the grace to lead a life of virtue, and that we may die a happy death, and attain eternal happiness. Amen.

Feast of the Nativity of the Blessed Virgin

Matt. i, 1–16

Let Us Rejoice at Mary's Happy Birth

> "Mary, of whom was born Jesus, who is called Christ."
> Matt. i, 16.

DEAR BRETHREN: To-day, the Church invokes the Blessed Virgin in these words: "O Mary who has borne God, thy birth has caused joy to the whole world." Joy in the house of the happy parents, Joachim and Anna, whose prayers God had answered in such a wondrous manner; joy in Heaven because the Eternal Father had predestined this child to be the Mother of His only Begotten Son; joy amongst the angels who received Mary as their gracious Queen; joy on earth amongst the just who received in her a tender, admirable Mother; joy amongst sinners who possess in Mary the Mother of mercy, their most assured refuge.

Therefore, it is at once our joy and our duty as children, dear Brethren, to rejoice to-day at the birth of our dearest Mother. Hence let us ask ourselves these questions:

I. Why was this day so blessed for Mary?

II. Is it a blessed day for us also?
The day of her birth was for Mary:

I. THE BEGINNING OF HER EXALTED OFFICE

God had given to Eve also a high office, and therefore she was as Queen of Paradise royally adorned with all holiness, righteousness, grace, and the love of God. According to her office she should be the Mother of the living, and should win all men for Heaven. But alas! through that first sin, she became the mother of the dead, and lost Heaven for us.

Far otherwise was it with Mary. She was appointed by God to be the Mother of the living, and to be the gate of Paradise for all mankind because she has given us the Redeemer. She was the Temple of God, purer than the Heavens, the Mother of the Lord. Mary was the woman who crushed the serpent's head; fair as the dawn of morning, beautiful as the moon, predestined as the sun, terrible as an army in battle-array against the enemies of our salvation. Behold the exalted office to which Mary was called for the greater Glory of God, and man's assistance.

2. Dear Brethren, we too at our birth have

had a heavy task imposed on us. God has given you life that you may enter into the service of the Lord, that your whole life may be a sowing for the great harvest, a day of preparation for Eternity. You must employ all your faculties for the glory of God and the salvation of your soul; you must lift yourself out of the mire; you must keep God's Commandments, and so merit eternal salvation.

II. THE BEGINNING OF A PAINFUL CONFLICT

1. Although Mary was a daughter of the royal house of David, yet she lived a life of poverty in an obscure little village. Although blessed amongst women, she was obliged to fly into Egypt and to dwell there amongst heathens until Herod was dead; in Nazareth she worked as the mother and the servant for the Holy Family. During the three years of Our Lord's Public Life, she had to listen to the blasphemies of His enemies who said He had a devil, who called Him a Sabbath-breaker, a seducer of the people. Then our Lord's awful Passion and Death! Who can comprehend Mary's sufferings. Is she not indeed the Queen of Martyrs?

2. Dear Brethren, in this our life here on earth

our vocation also, is to suffer. As gold is tried in the furnace, so is virtue tried in sorrow. Hence, our portion here on earth is poverty, sickness, temptation, thorns and thistles.

Had not Christ to suffer and so to enter into His Glory? So it is with us. Be faithful unto death and I will give you the crown of everlasting life. Without a fight there can be no victory, without victory there can be no crown.

Thus it is that we rejoice, dear Brethren, with the Blessed Virgin on this most joyous Feast of her happy Nativity, for Mary has conquered in the bitterest trials of her life. Therefore, before the Throne of God there ascends eternally her Magnificat: "My soul doth magnify the Lord . . . Because he that is mighty hath done great things to me: and holy is his name."

And as we rejoice with Mary, let us pray to her. O Mary, obtain for us thy children, God's grace that we may faithfully fulfill our vocation as Christians, may preserve our faith and may, with Thee surely attain the crown of Eternal Life. Amen.

FEASTS OF THE SAINTS AND MARTYRS

Feast of the First Martyr
ST. STEPHEN

Gospel, Matt. xxiii, 36–39
Epist., Acts vi, 8–10, 54–60

Witness for Christ

"Lord, Jesus, receive my spirit." Acts vii, 58.

DEAR BRETHREN: St. Stephen, whose great Feast we celebrate to-day, was not only the first of the seventy-two disciples of our Lord and the first amongst the seven deacons who were intrusted by the Apostles with the care of the churches and of the poor, to seal his testimony for Jesus Christ with his blood, but he was also the first martyr of the Church.

There are two beautiful lessons to be learnt from the martyrdom of St. Stephen; let us learn them and try to put them into practice.

I. ST. STEPHEN SAW THE HEAVENS OPEN

St. Luke in the Acts of the Apostles, tells us that "Stephen was full of grace and fortitude, did great wonders and signs among the people." He everywhere defended the truth of the Religion of Jesus Christ, and when he preached, his face shone like the face of an angel. He refuted all the arguments of the Pharisees against the divinity of Jesus Christ and converted many Jews to the Christian Faith.

But he said to the impious Jews: " you always resist the Holy Ghost." He told them that they betrayed and murdered the Messiah, and that thereby they had filled up the measure of their iniquities. At these words his enemies gnashed their teeth at him, and would fain have rushed upon him. Then Stephen, looking up to Heaven, cried aloud: " Behold, I see the Heavens opened, and the Son of Man standing on the right hand of God."

At these words, they flew into a violent rage, and stopped their ears.

Dear Brethren, how much we have to learn from this! Never be ashamed of being the disciples of Jesus Christ, but always fearlessly acknowledge your Religion; obey the Commandments of the Church; do not fear scoffs or jeers; do not keep silence when modern pagans condemn everything holy, but bravely defend the honor of God and the Name of Jesus; then will Jesus Christ acknowledge you for His own before His Heavenly Father and the angels.

But woe to those who in this life are ashamed to be followers of Jesus and faithful Christians. On the day of Judgment a fearful fate will overtake them.

II. STEPHEN PRAYED FOR HIS MURDERERS

Glorious as was the testimony rendered to the truth of the divine Religion of Jesus Christ by St. Stephen's life of angelic purity and by his splendid defence of that Religion, this testimony was rendered still more glorious by his holy death.

After his sermon the hardened Jews rushed at him, dragged him outside the city, tore from him his garments, pelted him with a perfect hail of stones, whilst Stephen, kneeling down, raised his eyes to Heaven and cried aloud, "Lord Jesus receive my spirit . . . Lord, lay not this sin to their charge." Stephen, like the Eternal Son of God on the Cross, pardoned his murderers who were stoning him to death, and thus proved himself a true disciple of Jesus Christ

FEASTS OF THE SAINTS AND MARTYRS

Who has said: "Love your enemies; do good to them that hate and persecute you."

His prayer was not unavailing; it did violence, as it were, to God, and had as its greatest and most wonderful fruit, the conversion of Saul who from being a fierce persecutor of the Church became its most zealous defender and the great Apostle Paul.

Dear Brethren, learn from Stephen who gave testimony to Christ in his blood, to be true Christians. The just man will not die at enmity with anyone; he will carry no feelings of hatred or resentment to the tomb; during his life, he will pardon his enemies quickly before the going down of the sun. This is the fairest flower of Christian Charity; this is to imitate the example of Jesus Christ in truth, of the Heavenly Father Himself Who delivered His only Begotten Son for the just and for sinners, Who in His Mercy, sent His divine Son into this world as our Redeemer, and thereby imposed on us as the condition of our own pardon, that we should pardon others.

St. Stephen obtain for us from Jesus the grace that we may do good to them that hate us, and pray for those that persecute us, that we may become heirs to that eternal happiness which Our Lord has promised to the meek and the peacemakers. Amen.

Feast of St. Joseph

Matt. i, 18–21

Our Protector

> "Thou shalt be over my house." Gen. xli, 40.

Dear Brethren: We all hold pious, good men in honor; how much greater veneration then, should we have for St. Joseph whom Jesus Christ Himself honored, and to whom He was obedient. As is indeed right and fitting, St. Joseph is everywhere held in the highest honor, the deepest reverence, and he has been declared the universal Patron and Protector of the Church. No Catholic Church, no Catholic house should be without its picture or statue of St. Joseph.

We implore the protection of St. Joseph as:

I. THE MOST CHASTE SPOUSE OF MARY

The most Blessed Virgin was not amongst those Jewish maidens who were dowered with wealth, but her dowry was richer, more precious than all earthly treasures; her heart was pure, immaculate, God's abiding place, the home of every virtue.

Mary, so richly dowered with every grace and virtue was espoused to Joseph who sought not riches nor earthly goods, but only to be espoused to a maiden rich in virtue that through her he might, with God's blessing, lead a holy life and die a happy death. These Spouses were of the most unsullied purity, and valued purity of soul and body above all else. Can we not imagine with what approval the Lord beheld the betrothal of Mary and Joseph?

O! Christian youths and maidens, to you do I address myself: Be modest; be virtuous; lead lives of Christian holiness, and value your baptismal innocence more than all the wealth of the world, more than all its honors, its pleasures. Of what avail would the possession of the whole world be to you, if by sin you lost your God, the highest Good. O! that all young people would not marry too young. Oh! that they would, by their virtue and modesty prepare themselves to enter into the married state.

II. ST. JOSEPH, THE TENDER FOSTER FATHER OF CHRIST AND GUARDIAN OF THE HOLY FAMILY

How did St. Joseph act when the Heavenly Father confided to his care the holiest on earth, Jesus and Mary? Although he had to bear the greatest poverty, to suffer Herod's persecution, he never murmured, but humbly adored the Will of God. He labored late and early to earn bread for the divine Child and His Mother; he did not blame the dispensations of divine Providence because he had to earn that bread in hardship and suffering whilst so many rich people were steeped in luxury, although he was of the royal house of David and in nobility of birth far above them. His was not only a labor of love but that labor became the service of God, for whilst he worked with his hands, his heart was united with God, with Jesus, wherefore every drop of his sweat became as a precious pearl and was carried by the angels to the throne of God. Jesus could have had the angels to serve Him and they would have brought Him all the necessaries of life in overflowing abundance. But it pleased His divine Wisdom to live by the labor of Joseph, His foster-father. St. Joseph was not ashamed to

FEASTS OF THE SAINTS AND MARTYRS 277

work, although he was of noble origin. Ah! how many young people fall into habits of idleness, go astray and become wretched ne'er-do-wells, and often the greatest criminals; for idleness is the parent of all vice, "if any man will not work neither let him eat," says St. Paul.[1] "Go to the ant, O sluggard, and consider her ways and learn wisdom."[2]

III. ST. JOSEPH, OUR ASSURED AID AT THE HOUR OF DEATH

In the hour of death we shall all need the protection of St. Joseph. He had the great privilege of giving up his soul to God in the arms of Jesus and Mary, and we hope, through his intercession to obtain the grace of a happy death. The Church encourages us in this hope by her approval of the Confraternity established in honor of St. Joseph for a happy death. The Church also honors St. Joseph on two special Feasts.

As a man lives, so will he die. Let us therefore, follow St. Joseph's example by leading a devout life, and we too shall also die a happy death. Amen.

---

[1] Thess. iii, 10.   [2] Prov. vi, 6.

278 BRIEF DISOCURSES ON THE GOSPELS

Feast of the Apostles Sts. Peter and Paul

Matt. xvi, 13–19

The Princes of the Church

"The just man liveth by faith." Rom. i, 17.

Dear Brethren: On this day, we should offer our most fervent thanksgiving to Almighty God, Who in His infinite Mercy has bestowed upon us from our birth the most precious gift of faith. And it was through the medium of the Princes of the Apostles, St. Peter and St. Paul, that the Christian Faith was first preached to the world. It is to these great Saints and Martyrs that we owe the preaching of the Faith; they are, therefore, our spiritual Fathers, and still to-day, our Teachers.

I. PETER, THE IMPREGNABLE ROCK ON WHOM THE CHURCH IS BUILT

When Jesus Christ put to the poor fisherman, Simon, the question, "But whom do you say I am?" enlightened by the Eternal Father, Simon Peter in his answer proclaimed the great Truth " Thou art Christ, the Son of the living God."

Whereupon, our divine Redeemer rewarded him for this proclamation of his faith in these words: "Blessed art thou, Simon Bar-jona: because flesh and blood hath not revealed it to thee, but my Father Who is in heaven. And I say to thee: That thou art Peter; and upon this rock I will build my church, and the gates of hell shall not prevail against it."

And never yet since those words were spoken, have the united forces of the enemies of God prevailed against the Catholic Church, neither unbelievers nor heretics, bad Catholics nor the devil himself. Therefore, let us ever steadfastly adhere to the successor of St. Peter, to the Holy Father the divinely appointed Head of Christ's Church on earth and thus we shall never waver in our faith or fall into error.

St. Peter is not only the rock upon which the Church on earth has been built, but he is also the Keeper of the Keys of the gates of Heaven. "And I will give to thee the keys of the kingdom of heaven. And whatsoever thou shalt bind upon earth, it shall be bound also in heaven: and whatsoever thou shalt loose on earth, it shall be loosed also in heaven."

The Eternal Son of God has given to Peter and his successors supreme authority over His Church. He has given them the power to decree and to forbid, to remit sins, or to reserve forgiveness; in a word, He has given them power to apply God's grace and mercy to all men who would find salvation. Therefore, dear Brethren, thank God unceasingly that He had made you members of His Church and draw water, with joy, from this Fountain of your eternal salvation.

II. PAUL, THE VESSEL OF ELECTION

"But by the grace of God, I am what I am; and his grace in me hath not been void." Thus did St. Paul make public confession, he who as a Jew had persecuted the Christians, but who being converted by Jesus Christ Himself, became the valiant Apostle of divine Truth, who, undergoing countless persecutions and sufferings, converted many nations, and finally like St. Peter, won the martyr's crown in Rome.

2. Dear Brethren, you, also, have been chosen from amongst millions of pagans to be children of the Catholic Church. Be grateful; be true children of the Church in whom all the fountains of salvation, of the Truth and Mercy of God are open to you. Never let your faith be torn from you; live as good Catholics that so at the end of your life, with St. Paul, you may

be able to say: "I have fought a good fight, I have finishd my course, I have kept the faith. As to the rest, there is laid up for me a crown of justice, which the Lord the just judge will render to me in that day."

Feast of the Guardian Angels
Matt. xviii, 1–10
Devotion to our Guardian Angels

> "For He hath given His Angels charge over thee; to keep thee in all thy ways."
> Ps. xc, 11.

DEAR BRETHREN: Amongst the greatest proofs of God's mercy is the teaching of the Church that He has given to us the holy angels for our service and protection; it is equally a proof of how precious are our immortal souls. An angel stands at my side, one of the Princes of Heaven accompanies me along the whole of life's road; a guardian spirit sent by God defends my soul against the attacks of the forces of Hell. How consoling this truth! What gratitude it calls for from us to God and to our Guardian Angels.

But not alone in words and devout prayers should our gratitude be shown, but also in deeds, in our holy lives.

1. What an incentive to good is the thought: I have at my side as witness of all my actions a pure angel who rejoices at my conversion and at all that I do of good; who praises God with me, and carries my prayers and good works to the Throne of God. How could I ever do wrong in his presence, how dare to despise, to make angry, to lead astray a fellow-creature beside whom also stands an Angel of God?

Dear Brethren, surely we dare not do anything at which our good angel must weep.

2. What a consolation in all our needs of soul and body! My Guardian Angel supports my prayers; obtains grace for me; speaks to me through my conscience; exhorts me; warns me, helps me to combat the Evil One. What a good friend! A friend who will remain faithful to my last breath that he may lead me into Paradise!

How consoling for those parents who know that their children are in danger! how consoling indeed for all mankind who are continually exposed to danger!

But this service of love which our guardian angels render us demands in return our true devotion and reverence.

3. We should imitate our guardian angels. *We should be angels* ourselves.

(*a*) Angels of Prayer. The angels serve God by perpetual adoration in deepest reverence before His Throne. If we now are also adoring angels we may hope to join them in their adoration throughout Eternity.

(*b*) Angels of Obedience. The angels ever do the Will of God—promptly, punctually, exactly, for this reason they are represented with wings. So should you serve God, fulfil punctually your duties not because of men, but to glorify God. Do not be dissatisfied with your position; do not murmur or complain, but obey with angelic love.

(*c*) Angels of Purity. Oh! how beautiful is a pure creature, resplendent in virtue! Such a one is beloved of God and man. How hateful is the opposite vice! Shun every danger and occasion of sin. Honor Mary, the Queen of Angels; implore of her "Through thy sacred virginity and Immaculate Conception, O most chaste Virgin, obtain for me purity of soul and body." In all places, no matter how retired, remember the presence of your Guardian Angel. Take care that he may never become your accuser, but rather may be ever your advocate.

(d) The Children's Guardian Angels. God loves the innocent. Jesus calls the little ones to Him, promises them the Kingdom of Heaven, and blesses all those who receive a child in His name. But He also pronounces a curse on those who scandalise an innocent child.

Dear Brethren, return thanks to-day to the Heavenly Father for having in His Goodness given us the holy angels to serve us that we may under their protection so much more easily attain Eternal Life. And strive by your zealous imitation of the angelic virtues to deserve their protection. Amen.

FEAST OF ALL SAINTS
Matt. vi, 1-12
" Praise God in His Saints"

Ps. cl, 1.

DEAR BRETHREN: The first word which our divine Savior in this day's Gospel says to us is: "Blessed!" yes "Blessed!" Could He begin in a manner better adapted to secure the attention of His hearers than by promising them eternal happiness? Varied as are the thoughts and desires of men, yet there is one desire which we all have—the desire to be eternally happy.

And Jesus has taught us all the ways and the means by which we may attain happiness, of which all God's Saints have diligently made use to reach their goal of eternal happiness.

In order, dear Brethren, that we may be induced to imitate the Saints, the Church has appointed this great Feast of all Saints. Let us consider briefly the instructive meaning of this Feast.

1. Before all, this Feast sets before us the victory of Christianity over paganism. The heathen gods were but the idealisation of the most abominable vices into which mankind had fallen. The Saints were the most perfect examples of heroic virtue; the heathens lay in the darkness of superstition; the Church shone in the light of faith and instead of the awful sacrifices to idols, she offered the sacrifice of the spotless Lamb, Jesus Christ. Under heathenism Satan made slaves of free nations; under Christianity Jesus Christ raised men to be children of God.

2. The Feast of all Saints has for its justification the saying " Honor to whom honor is due." We know that God Himself glorifies all His Saints—by the most wonderful miracles on earth, and by the greatest rewards in Heaven. Therefore, it is fitting that we also should honor

the Saints, invoke them, imitate their virtues and praise God in His faithful servants, because, indeed all their works of virtue are only the effect of His divine Grace. Therefore David sings "Praise God in His Saints."

3. And how consoling is it to look up to such countless advocates. "But to me thy friends, O God," says David, "are made exceedingly honorable: their principality is exceedingly strengthened." If indeed the prayer of the just here on earth avails much, how much more powerful must be the prayer of a glorified friend of God. If indeed, the devout on earth pray much for one another, how could the Saints in Heaven be unmindful of their brothers and sisters.

4. But the imitation of the Saints is the crown of our veneration and invocation of them. Our lives should be in harmony with those things which we admire in them. Jesus Christ tells us, "Be ye perfect as your heavenly Father is perfect." And St. Paul says: "Be ye followers of me, as I also am of Christ."

And millions of Saints, "a great multitude, whom no man could number, of all nations, and tribes, and peoples, and tongues," repeat the words of St. Paul.

That we may be encouraged to do this, St. Augustine says, "If this one and that one could do such things, why not I also?"

Oh! how beautiful is the Church, truly, a tree which has borne good fruit and ever produces such. How many pure hearts, how many just men, how many merciful Christians, how many patient, meek, humble servants of God who persevering unto death, have in the Church won the prize of eternal happiness.

My Brethren, do you also fight the good fight; preserve your faith; beg of God the grace of perseverance in doing good that by imitating the Saints you may, after this short life, be received into their glorious company. Amen.